Radiance 4 Life

THE 4 CORNERSTONES OF ULTIMATE VITALITY

Radiance 4 Life

THE 4 CORNERSTONES OF ULTIMATE VITALITY

Tess Challis

Published by Quintessential Health Publishing
P.O. Box 1784
Pagosa Springs, CO 81147
www.RadiantHealth-InnerWealth.com

Printed in the United States of America
First edition 2011

Food photograph on the front cover:
"Fresh Shiitake Sesame Spring Rolls" by Olga Vasiljeva

Food photographs on the back cover (left to right):
"Spicy Moroccan Sweet Potato Fries," "Raw Cinnamon Rolls," "Fresh and Fast Thai Tofu Bowl," and "Hungarian Chickpeas" by Olga Vasiljeva

ISBN: 978-1463557201

This book is dedicated to *you.*
May it inspire and empower you to live a life of radiant vitality!

In Gratitude

I've said it once and I'll say it again—there's no way I could ever do what I do without lots of support! First of all, I would like to thank my mother, Kathryn Barnes, who was my first natural foods teacher. Thanks also to my uncle, Mark Challis, for being an inspiring role model for lifelong vegetarianism. My grandma, Patricia Challis, also deserves many thanks for helping me through college, where I first began to study holistic health and nutrition.

I owe Sheila Barrows a debt of gratitude for being such a brilliant editor—and for her immense generosity and patience in this department!

I also owe many thanks to my beloved recipe testers. Because of their feedback, each recipe is better than it would have been without their input. Many thanks to Erica Hunter, Tracy Riley, Stacey Groth, Jan Nicolet, Leslie Conn, Diana Cook, Karen Fuller, Steve Fuller, Chris Humphrey, Diane April, Diana Cook, Sam Moorhead, Jan Moorhead, Nastassja Riley, Anastacia Norris, Janet Malowany, and Alice Gilbert. Thanks also to Charles Ferebee for his very helpful contributions. I appreciate you all!

I also feel so grateful to Robert Cheeke, Lindsay S. Nixon, Dreena Burton, Dr. Neal Barnard, and Jill Eckart. Despite all of their extremely busy schedules, they somehow found the time to review this book and I am truly thankful for that!

And as usual, the talented Olga Vasiljeva is due a debt of gratitude for enthusiastically taking such beautiful food photographs for me. Seriously, someone please hire her and pay her tons of money—she is amazing!

Finally, I would like to thank every single person who has ever told me that they changed their diet and/or life due to reading my books. You have no idea how much all of your positive feedback means to me. It really does keep me going!

Thanks so much. You are all deeply, deeply appreciated!

Foreword

In **Radiance 4 Life**, you will be inspired by the way Tess outlines the cornerstones that constitute a healthy, enriching, and truly radiant life. Focused on the key elements that matter the most in our pursuit of health—eating a plant-based diet, exercising, inner wellness, and consuming superfoods, Tess prepares you for a vibrant future.

Complete with food preparation guidance, recipes, and menu suggestions, this book is sure to bring out your very best in culinary creativity for ultimate health and vitality.

As a champion bodybuilder and vegan for more than a decade and a half, I have lived by these very cornerstones of health in my own journey to achievement. Without the complimentary component of fitness to support a balanced plant-based diet, the penultimate in health still lingers without completeness. When combined, a whole-food plant-based diet rich in superfoods—supported by exercise—gives you the greatest chance to live a long, fulfilling life to pursue your passions unique to you and your interests. A healthy lifestyle inside and out supports any ambition, while reducing the risk of illness and disease.

With mouth-watering recipes and meal plans fit for a King or Queen, you'll feel like one yourself as you turn each new page to find another soup, salad, entrée, or sweet dish to salivate over. Plus, you'll feel empowered by Tess's clear instructions to prepare these royal meals for yourself, your friends, and your family.

Written from the heart with enthusiasm, Tess speaks to all of us in a language that is the most universal and understood by all; the language of love. Eating for optimal health and sharing that with those you care about is an expression of love, appreciation, and hope for a brighter, more vibrant and radiant future. Look no further than the exercise tips with bullet points shaped as hearts to know Tess is writing from hers.

In **Radiance 4 Life**, you will learn to "love thyself," to visualize and breathe your way to inner health, and to discover how to make superfoods delicious. You will be equipped to take on the world . . . or the kitchen, the weekend picnic in the park, or monthly vegan potluck. Embrace the "Superstar" foods, as Tess describes them, and use these foods to enhance the creativity and nutrition of your daily meal plans.

Radiant recipes with innovative themes blanket the pages of this book with inspiring dishes. Tess includes gluten-free, soy-free, raw, and even "green" and "blue" dishes, as well as those which can be prepared in under 30 minutes. Whether you're in the mood for "Power Pancakes" like me, or an "Eye Love You Smoothie," you'll be back to say, "Maca My Day" to the next scrumptious recipe.

Do yourself a favor and try these wonderful, delicious, health-giving recipes. Share some "Zesty Lemon Kale Chips" with your family and see who's lining up for "Vegan Cheese Sticks" or "Spicy Moraccan Sweet Potato Fries." These are a healthier alternative to the unhealthy options that are the mainstay in the diets of many.

The cornerstones of radiant health can be achieved by all of us. They are the universal truths that bond us together as compassionate individuals determined to make the world a better place in one collective effort to achieve global peace and wellness.

Nourish yourself, your family, and your friends and loved ones around the world—one delicious bite, one early morning run, one soothing deep breath, one "Strawberry Vanilla Milkshake," and one radiant smile at a time.

- Robert Cheeke, best-selling author of *Vegan Bodybuilding & Fitness - The Complete Guide to Building Your Body on a Plant-Based Diet*

Contents

Introduction

Ultimate vitality—quite a lofty concept, right? Yes, I do realize that this idea conjures up phrases like "pie-in-the-sky perfection" and images of superhero capes. However, ultimate vitality is not only attainable, it's also probable if you follow the four main concepts in this book. In fact, it doesn't even have to be difficult once you get going! To create your very own self-maintaining structure of ultimate vitality, all you need to do is make sure your cornerstones are in place.

What exactly are these cornerstones? First of all, it's highly beneficial to eat a balanced plant-based diet. And although this might sound challenging, I assure you that healthy vegan (plant-based) food is varied and sublimely delicious—plus, the health benefits are astounding! Additionally, your chances of living a long, completely disease-free life are almost guaranteed if you do so. Isn't that exciting? Think of Loreen Dinwiddie who just celebrated her 108th birthday. She's been vegan since 1922 and says she doesn't even experience aches and pains!

The second cornerstone is inner wellness. We simply cannot expect to be holistically healthy unless we're balanced within ourselves. Fortunately, creating a foundation of inner wellness and peace is actually an enjoyable, rewarding journey. All it requires is the willingness to "go within" on a regular basis and realize the peace and abundance that is part of your essential nature. Our natural state is one of total peace, but if we neglect our inner wellness it's easy to forget that simple fact. By nurturing the self within, we will easily regain balance, peace, and joy.

The third cornerstone is exercise. If we want to experience wellness on all levels, it's important to move it and groove it! Exercise can be enjoyable, natural, and sustainable—all it takes is a little planning and perseverance.

Finally, the fourth cornerstone is eating a superfood-rich diet—and this is where the fun really gains momentum! In this book, you'll discover a whole new world of delicious, vitalizing plant-based superfoods that will delight your palate and nourish your body. Still thinking a vegan diet is boring? Whip up a batch of "Rawcho Cheese Dip," "Asparagus Walnut Sunshine Salad," "Feel Fabulous Noodles," and "Key Lime Pie with Coconut Ginger Crust." If you don't think they're just about the best things you've ever eaten, let me know and I'll buy you something nice.

So, what exactly is ultimate vitality? I define it as being totally in balance and aligned with our natural state of complete wellness. In other words, it's not something unattainable—it's actually our fundamentally natural state of being. We were born to be radiantly healthy, happy, and peaceful. I truly believe this and have observed it countless times in my own life. The only time I'm not feeling it is when I do something out of alignment and get in my own way. But when I'm eating properly (according to the simple guidelines on p. 8-9), exercising, and taking care of my inner wellness needs, ultimate vitality just happens. I don't have to force it or try to attain it. It just is. And it's beautiful. We are all children of the Divine and have so much potential, right at our very fingertips! However, we have listened too long to so-called educators who have made a basic state of wellness seem unattainable—or at least, quite expensive.

However, this simply is not so—all you need to do to experience ultimate vitality is replace unhealthy habits with nourishing habits, such as the four cornerstones in this book. Go at your own pace and build a solid foundation of wellness for yourself, remembering that Rome wasn't built in a day. If you consistently take positive actions (such as trying new recipes from this book, exercising more, and paying more attention to your inner wellness needs), you'll find that your persistence really will pay off. You'll begin to awaken into a higher level of living—one that feeds you body, mind, and soul. You will begin to realize that you really don't have to give up anything and that you only gain by implementing these cornerstones.

Finally, I'd like to ask you to take a moment—right now in the middle of the bookstore or bathtub—and ask yourself who exactly it is that you'd ideally like to become. Open yourself up to what you truly desire and try not to limit yourself. Do you long for a zen-like state of inner peace? Do you want to have movie-star triceps and glowing skin? Do you want to overcome existing health problems, feel better, and have boundless energy? No matter what your goals, the cornerstones in this book will help you make them happen. So, set aside any preconceived ideas of what you can achieve and open your mind to a new reality—one of infinite potential! Because the truth is, ultimate vitality *is* within your reach. You absolutely can be the best version of yourself, both internally and externally, without losing a single thing! And I wish you infinite joy, inspiration, and empowerment on your journey.

Cornerstone One:
Eating a Balanced Plant-Based Diet

Before we go any further, can I just say that I realize how boring a "balanced plant-based diet" might sound to you? Given the images this conjures up for many of us (plain steamed broccoli and lima beans, anyone?), it's no surprise. However, I also know for a fact that it's anything but boring in reality.

So, what makes this way of eating, in fact, totally exciting? People are usually surprised when I tell them that there are literally thousands of delicious options in the realm of plant-based foods. In fact, do you know what the most common thing I hear is when someone begins a vegan (plant-based) diet? They invariably tell me that the new foods are more exciting, varied, and delicious than anything they were previously eating. Just take a gander through the recipes in this book and I know you'll agree!

The Basics

A plant-based diet is one that excludes all animal products. So, this means no more lard, chicken, fish, red meat, eggs, dairy, or any products that may include them. I know that throws up red flags for many of us, especially when we've been eating these foods since childhood. However, we must also realize that animal foods contain no fiber, raise our cholesterol, and greatly contribute to many illnesses and diseases. Just by eschewing animal foods, you will add many years onto your life and greatly reduce your risk for cancer, heart disease, obesity, diabetes, and so many other prevalent problems that plague our society.

However, my approach isn't just about eating a vegan diet. It's about eating a supremely **healthy** vegan diet. So, in addition to saying goodbye to animal foods, I also recommend eliminating (or at least reducing) refined foods, excessive sweeteners, artificial ingredients, hydrogenated oils, and processed foods.

I know what you're thinking. "What's left? I'm a-gonna starve!" I know, it sounds really restrictive. But I promise you, it's not—not at all. And in fact, once you get used to this new way of eating, you'll feel more thrilled about what's on your plate than ever before. It's just a matter of readjusting your taste buds, discovering a new world of scrumptious foods, and being turned on to the vitalizing results of this way of eating.

However, despite the impending deliciousness that awaits you in the plant-based world, I realize that for many of you this may still sound overwhelming. I understand—I too felt overwhelmed when I first considered this prospect. "What will I eat? Won't I miss the old foods? What about pepperoni pizza and Taco Bell?" These were all thoughts that genuinely concerned me many years ago. But can I suggest something? Perhaps if the thought of forever giving up these foods makes you want to run for the hills, you can use another approach—and that approach is to just *try* it.

In fact, this was what I did twenty years ago. I gave myself two weeks to "just see." I had no idea at the time, though, that I would feel better than ever and love the food so darned much. And what happened when those two weeks were up? I had no interest in adding the animal foods back into my diet. It was no longer a question of will power. I didn't have to force myself to eat a vegan diet. It came naturally from a place of love and fulfillment. And honestly, from being a foodie! I know it sounds odd, but the truth is that I never enjoyed food as much as an omnivore as I have as a vegan. Properly prepared plant-based foods are absolutely delicious, as you will soon see. A vegan diet truly is a win-win—and then some!

However, I understand that we're all different. If it's difficult for you to give up animal foods all at once, I'd like to again suggest that you simply try it. Try it in whatever way you can, keeping in mind that you're creating a healthy foundation that you can continually improve on. Do your best and don't judge yourself. Keep having fun in the kitchen while you're trying new vegan recipes. Because it's not about being perfect—it's about a continual state of improvement. You really can be the healthiest, most radiant version of yourself. And if you do it at a pace that's truly sustainable for you, you'll be more likely to stick with it for life!

My Journey

Back when I first started eating a strictly plant-based diet in 1991, I had no idea what an amazing, life changing event I was becoming a part of. It all started in college, while I was living with a new friend, Anne. I had already been vegetarian for a year (while consuming eggs and dairy), but couldn't help noticing that Anne simply radiated vitality and health. Once I found out that she was vegan, I remember being surprised—how did she stay so healthy, despite the lack of animal products in her diet? The more I got to know her (and observe the fascinating things she ate), the more interested I became in a plant-based diet.

Before long, I began researching vegan diets. I was utterly shocked and excited to find out that a vegan diet represented a supremely nourishing way of eating, and that any fears I'd had about it were a result of being educated by advertisements for so many years. Everything I had taken as facts before (such as the four food groups) were actually just advertisements, either by the Dairy Council or some other animal agriculture businesses. So, I began my journey. Immediately, I noticed dramatic results—my skin cleared up, my chronic colds and bouts with strep throat were gone, my nails went from brittle to strong, my energy level went way up, and I felt fantastic.

Twenty years later, I'm loving a plant-based diet even more. The foods are scrumptious, the health benefits are fantastic, and I rest easier at night knowing that animals haven't had to give their lives to satisfy my taste buds. But to tell you the truth, I don't feel like it's a sacrifice in the least. I'm so fulfilled with this delicious variety of food that I can't imagine anything tasting better. One of my greatest joys is when I receive a letter from someone saying that they've turned their life and health around, simply by loving the delicious foods in my books. Can you tell how excited I get about this stuff? It's for good reason! There's just no need to suffer through life, eating foods that make us sick, and feeling helpless to do anything about it. We can easily and naturally readjust our palates to a new way of eating—one that not only satisfies our taste buds, but also keeps us feeling, looking, and functioning at our highest and most vibrant levels.

What Comprises a Supremely Vitalizing Vegan Diet?

So, now that you're inspired and excited, the question remains—what exactly should you eat on a vegan diet? Luckily, the answer is actually quite simple! If you follow my simple guidelines, you can't go wrong. Listed below is everything you'll ever need to know about eating an optimal, balanced vegan diet—in six easy steps.

1. *Emphasize whole foods.* What exactly does it mean to eat "whole foods?" It's a term we hear constantly, but many people are still unsure of its exact meaning. Whole foods are those plant-based foods that aren't altered (well, much) by humans. Some examples would be a whole potato (vs. potato chips), beans (vs. tofu), and brown rice (vs. pasta). Try to eat whole-grain, minimally processed foods as much as possible, as they will give you the most bang for your nutritional buck.

2. *Eat lots of superfoods!* Nature provided us with some pretty awesome stuff—maca for strength and endurance, blueberries for eyesight, and sweet potatoes for beautiful skin. Take advantage of the goodness and start working more and more superfoods into your diet. For more ideas on superfoods, read a book on the subject. Wait, you already are. Well done, you!

3. *Drink plenty of purified water.* Water will keep your digestive system functioning properly, your weight down, and your skin glowing. Aim for a bare minimum of half of your body weight in ounces daily—but if possible, drink more than that for optimal results. Incidentally, you can make sun tea using nutrient-dense additions such as nettles, raspberry leaf, mint, green tea, and hibiscus. It's the perfect way to stay hydrated and nutrified at the same time!

4. *Vitamin B-12* is the one and only precaution I recommend taking on a plant-based diet. However, this vitamin is stored in the body for long periods of time, so you don't need to take it every day. In fact, many experts say that you don't need to supplement with this vitamin at all. However, since there is contradicting advice on the subject, you might as well be on the safe side and take a little B-12 every once in a while. At the very least, it will make your mom happy.

5. *Vegetables—you just can't eat too many of them!* Literally, it's almost impossible. Veggies are *the* food to emphasize in your diet if you want gorgeous skin, excellent health, a strong immune system, and a healthy weight. Aim for at least five cups of fresh vegetables daily. It's also a good idea to think in terms of color—the more colors you eat, the more vitalizing your diet will be! The colors green (kale, parsley, lettuce, etc.) and orange (carrots, sweet potatoes, mangoes, etc.) are especially rich in antioxidants and nutrients.

6. *Don't overeat.* Eat less . . . the simplest advice, but so very important! Of course, this doesn't actually have to do with veganism, but since it's a crucial part of physical well-being, I wanted to include it here. The best way to incorporate this step into your life is to become aware—awareness truly is key! Become tuned into the exact moment when you've eaten enough. This moment occurs just after you've eaten enough to be physically satisfied, but before you're "full." You want to always leave a little room in your stomach—say 20%—to enjoy total wellness, a lightness of being, and maximum energy.

Cornerstone Two: Exercise

We've all heard it. And heard it. And heard it yet again—we need regular exercise to really get the full benefits of a healthy lifestyle. Exercise does all kinds of miraculous things. It improves our mood, helps us maintain a healthy weight, increases energy and vitality, and it even helps prevent chronic diseases and illnesses.

But unfortunately, too many of us have come to believe that exercise is the same as drudgery. We think we have to subject ourselves to painful routines that are anything but fun, in hopes that someday it will pay off. (Cue sad violins and images of people doing way too many stomach crunches in striped leotards.)

Well, my darlings, I am here to tell you something. And that is: There is no need to force yourself—ever—to participate in physical fitness activities that you don't like. In fact, it's my belief that this is why so many of us fail at really sticking with a healthy exercise routine long term.

As always, my approach is one of "doability." Not a word? Now it is! What really matters in the long run is how much you enjoy what you're doing and how likely it is that it will become a lifetime habit. What's the use of forcing yourself into a routine that you'll abandon after a few weeks, and then feel so guilty about it that you start eating chips and cookies to soothe yourself? No, no, and no! What we really need is a new approach—one that is simultaneously fun, effective, and realistic. ***Doable.***

That said, there really is a formula for the ideal exercise foundation. Any healthy, enjoyable, and truly successful fitness program has four main components. And believe me—if I can do it, so can you. I come from a long line of exercise haters. And I know that we most likely haven't met (yet), but trust me. I know you well enough to tell you your business. You really can rock the exercise world, starting now.

Principle One: Fun

Ah, fun. What could be more important in life? Well, maybe a few things. Water and love being two of them. But I gotta tell you, no matter how important the other stuff, it can always be improved with a big, fat, healthy dose of fun. Want to make your habits more natural and effortless to maintain in the long run? Just add fun! Aside from the obvious benefits you'll receive from exercise, wouldn't you just want to do it every day if you knew it would be fun and that you'd actually enjoy it?

So, ask yourself: What do you love to do? What kinds of exercise could you genuinely see yourself looking forward to on a regular basis? For me, asking this question was a major breakthrough in my exercise world. One day the idea just hit me: "Why don't I swear off—forever more—the idea that I have to do any exercise that I hate? I can create a very effective routine doing only exercises that I truly enjoy!"

For me, that meant saying goodbye to things I had previously forced myself to do (hence, things that made me less likely to want to exercise overall). And it made me focus instead on things I really loved. For me, that's a long list, including swimming, strength training, yoga, bike riding, walking, hiking, cross-country skiing, Nia, dancing, Pilates, and more.

Now, with all of those ways to actually enjoy fitness, why on earth was I forcing myself to do things I didn't like? In the same way we're taught to think about so many things (including what a healthy diet means), we unfortunately believe that we have to suffer in order to be fit.

Well, I'm here to tell you otherwise, my friends! We can all reach our ultimate healthy potential while eating delicious foods and creating a fun exercise routine that we can actually look forward to! All it takes is a little creativity, exploration, and self-love, and you too will be having a blast while simultaneously getting in the best shape of your life. And seriously, I'm not kidding—I really believe all of this sunshine stuff.

Fun Tips:

♥ Make a list of all of the enjoyable things you can do for exercise. These can either be things you're already familiar with, or things that you've never tried but always wanted to. Post your list somewhere visible so you can refer to it often for inspiration. And feel free to decorate your list with sparkly stickers and smiley faces.

♥ Find a workout buddy—preferably someone you like. From there, you can double your fun and even work out those abdominals with some great belly laughs!

♥ Include music. Studies show that we work out longer, become stronger, and get more results when we're listening to music we enjoy. Load up your music player with tunes that make it physically impossible to avoid shaking your booty.

♥ Have a dog? If so, you know what to do. Don't have a dog, but thinking you could give one a good home? Then check out your local rescue organization or shelter and adopt one. From there, you can have fun taking daily walks together. It'll do your heart (and your *heart*) good!

♥ Don't want to commit to having a dog of your own, but like the previous idea? Many shelters and rescue organizations welcome volunteers to walk dogs.

♥ Join a class. There are all kinds of great dance and exercise classes out there, and most are pretty reasonably priced. It's a great way to stay motivated, learn new things, meet interesting humans, and create variety in your routine. *Fun.*

Principle Two:
Stretch Your Body and Your Mind Will Follow

Stretching. Yes, it really is as important as all the health and yoga gurus have made it seem. When you stretch properly, you get more out of your workout in ever so many ways. First of all, stretching greatly increases your range of motion. This helps to increase your flexibility, while simultaneously decreasing your chance of injuries.

In addition, stretching increases the blood flow to your muscles and assists circulation. Stretching promotes a better energy flow throughout your whole body by removing blockages. Thus, stretching makes it possible (and legitimate) to say things like: "My chi is really flowing now, people."

By stretching properly, you'll experience less muscle tension, resulting in fewer incidences of soreness after exercise. Finally, stretching is a great way to bring more relaxation into your workout and your life. And when we're relaxed, every little thing just seems to work better and function at a higher level.

Stretching tips:

♥ Have you ever taken a yoga class? So simple, but so life changing! Also, don't be shy about trying out different instructors. Even after all the yoga classes I've taken over the years, I always—*always*—learn something new from every yoga teacher.

♥ Try fitting in little stretches throughout your exercise routine. Personally, when I do my strength building routine, I like to stretch after working each muscle group. So, for example, once I've worked on my calf muscles, I'll stretch them before moving on to the next muscle group.

♥ Before starting any exercise routine, warm up for five minutes (by walking, for example) and then do your stretches. This way, your body will be able to get much more out of each stretch. From there, you can begin your exercise routine.

♥ Don't bounce when you stretch. Forget what you learned in your 1980s aerobics class. The best way to stretch may indeed be to wear hot pink leg warmers, but don't bounce. A slow, steady stretch is always the best way to prevent injury and warm up your muscles.

♥ Try to breathe into your stretches. If you feel resistance anywhere, allow your focus and breath to flow to that place. And then just allow yourself to take a little more time and feel the stretch. Don't hurry. You'll get the best results from each stretch when you hold it a little longer. You'll also notice you can stretch further and further when you stay in the stretch longer and breathe consciously.

Principle Three: Build Muscle

Just in case you were worried, I will start off by saying that building muscle has nothing to do with becoming overly muscular. Rest assured that you can read the rest of this chapter knowing that you won't be asked to take up body building, drink protein shakes, or purchase tiny bathing suit bottoms to show off your bulging, shiny thighs.

What I'm talking about here is getting very strong and very toned. Plus, here's the really exciting part: As you build muscle, your metabolism increases, meaning that it's even easier to maintain a healthy weight and stay fit with less effort. True story! Isn't that exciting? Muscle really does burn more calories than fat, which means that our even our resting metabolism rate increases as our muscle tone increases. In other words, once you build muscle, you'll consistently burn more calories even when you're laying around being lazy (which is, incidentally, an important part of any balanced regime).

In fact, this is one of the main reasons why it's so important to include strength training in your exercise routine. Many people focus solely on cardiovascular exercise, not realizing that if they just spent some time building muscle, their fitness goals would become much more attainable. And just in case you were wondering, I don't care how old you are. I've seen people even in their eighties and nineties kicking butt and taking names in this department. Nothing excites me more than seeing an octogenarian rocking out with free weights.

So, what actually happens when we strength train? When we build muscle, we're creating small tears in the fibers of our muscle. I know it sounds weird, but it's actually how muscles are built. In fact, it's while we're in recovery (the times in between strength training) that our muscles repair and get stronger.

Thus, it's important not to overdo any strength training routine, especially at first. Usually, it's sufficient to strength train each muscle twice weekly. That gives you a few days in between sessions to recover and get stronger. In fact, you can even start by doing it just once per week. Remember, this is all about doable, sustainable steps that work for *you!*

So, I recommend that you set up a schedule that truly works for you. One that includes a minimum of one day per week for each muscle group. You can work with all of the muscle groups in one day, or spread them out if you prefer. For example, some people (like me) might do a complete strength training routine on Tuesdays and Fridays so that all the muscle groups are covered twice per week, while putting in a minimum of gym time.

However, others might prefer to do their upper body exercises on Mondays and Thursdays, while doing their lower body exercises on Tuesdays and Fridays. No matter what you choose, the most important thing is to give your muscles a chance to recover in between days so that you're not overworking them. Slow and steady wins the race!

Muscle building tips:

♥ Start with a doable plan. If that means once per week, then so be it. You are creating a solid foundation that you can continually build on. Think long term.

♥ Be sure to stretch before each exercise for maximum results and minimum chance of injuries. Plus, stretching just feels good. Why else would it be the highest ranking hobby of all cats?

♥ Consult a certified personal trainer—someone you enjoy working with and who listens to you. Even if you only do a few sessions, a good trainer can get you off to a powerful start and help you develop an effective routine.

♥ If you join a gym, you can often get a lot of free advice—some of which will even be useful. The employees will usually show you the proper way to use weight machines, and many will even give you tips on how to do free weight exercises properly. And of course there's always the guy in the muscle shirt telling you to tuck in your elbows and lift with your legs.

♥ Be sure to keep your body in alignment when you're strength training. If your body isn't in the correct position, you can strain or injure yourself.

♥ As always, have fun! Listen to music, enlist a buddy, and focus on exercises you enjoy (or at least don't hate!).

♥ Keep your focus on all of the improvements you're making. Take measurements, keep track of your progress, and notice how your physique and stamina are changing for the better. Look in the mirror and make obnoxious, sexist comments while whistling at yourself. In this context, political correctness is irrelevant.

Principle Four: Cardio (Cardiovascular exercise)

And now for the fun part! Good old fashioned cardio is what really gets our heart pumping, our energy up, and our mood skyrocketing. Endorphins much? Yes, please!

Plus, cardio can be all kinds of enjoyable. What's not to like about dancing, taking an evening walk, or cross-country skiing? There's also running, jogging, bike riding, walking, aerobics, Nia or Tae Bo, the elliptical machine or stair stepper at the gym, swimming, and hiking. Just to name a few. And even if you don't like the sound of most of these activities, I'm guessing there are one or two you could find a way to enjoy, right? That's where it all starts!

The ways to strengthen your heart and improve your immune system through cardiovascular exercise are practically unlimited. And here's another benefit—it's addictive! Once you get accustomed to a healthy exercise routine that includes plenty of cardio, you won't want to miss it.

Cardio tips:

♥ As in all things, I'm a big believer in keeping things doable and creating a solid foundation. Therefore, I recommend that you start with a minimum amount that you know you can stick with (such as 30 minutes, three times per week) and build on that. Basically, I want to read a letter from you six months from now, telling me how you slowly built up a fantastic exercise routine that you're now loving. I want you to overuse words like "jazzed."

♥ Fit in little bits of extra cardio throughout your day. All the seemingly insignificant stuff really does add up! For example, park further away, take the stairs, or even do a few jumping jacks here and there. Sure, people might think you're a little nutty. But at least you (and they) won't be bored!

♥ Start with a gentle warm-up (such as walking) for five minutes. Then stretch for several minutes before beginning your cardio routine.

♥ It's also important to cool down at the end of your session. This can be something as simple as walking or stretching for a few minutes. By the way, I'm terrible at this. If you see me at the gym, feel free to call me out on this one and rub in my face how much better you are than me in this department. I can take it.

♥ Want to reduce the guilt factor (not that I condone the useless emotion of guilt, that is!) while you're watching a movie? Place a recumbent bike or treadmill in your living room and work your body while giving your brain a rest. Unless, of course, you're watching a movie that actually makes you think— which has been known to happen in rare cases. Still, I'm guessing you're the kind of person who can exercise, think, and even chew gum at the same time.

♥ Do you live within walking (or biking) range of any businesses you frequent? If so, you can simultaneously save money, get fit, and make a gentler impact on the environment. Right on, crouton!

So, my friends, there you have it—the four basic principles that will have you feeling and looking even more fantastic through the magic of exercise. I wish you much fun and empowerment on your journey to greater and greater wellness. May you continually surprise yourself!

Cornerstone Three: Inner Wellness

"Anywhere is paradise; it's up to you." -Anonymous

This quote perfectly illustrates why the concept of inner wellness is so very important. If we can create and maintain an inner core of well-being, then we can find peace and happiness anywhere we are. We can find it anywhere because we take it with us **everywhere**. Once you build that foundation of inner wellness, it is always within you—nurturing you, making your own life better in every way, and improving the lives of all those you come into contact with. I know it might sound overly simplistic, but it's true. Building a foundation of inner well-being is the one thing that will make everything else in your life blossom. I know it because I've seen it happen continually in my own life. Simply put, it works!

So, what exactly is inner wellness? In a nutshell, it's a feeling of peace, love, joy, compassion, understanding, and well-wishing for everyone—including yourself. It's a state of mind that trusts in the divine perfection of the Universe and knows that we're all in this together—so why not help each other, live in joy, and be happy? For the better each of us feels within our own being, the more we can lift others up as well.

I know this concept may be new to many of you—we're taught from childhood to ignore our inward state. However, no matter at what age we begin, it's never too late to learn some basic inner wellness skills. It doesn't even have to be difficult— it can be a path of joy, wonder, and relaxation. I would like to encourage you to take your time, go at your own pace, and develop an inner wellness regime that is doable for you in your life right now. Review the tools in this chapter (visualization, meditation, and self-love) and use them to formulate a personalized routine for yourself that you can build on.

No matter what tools you choose to begin with, please remember that every little bit counts. No matter how hard it might be in the beginning, know that it really does get easier and more enjoyable the more you do it! Be kind and gentle with yourself, and don't forget to have fun and nurture yourself in the process.

Visualization

"Worry is a misuse of imagination." -Dan Zadra

I so love this quote! It's the perfect example of how most of us use one of the most powerful tools we have at our fingertips—our imagination. Unfortunately, we so often forget that what we think about in our mind is what we create in our life. We spend our time worrying about the future, not realizing that we're creating more of the same by focusing on what we ***don't*** want.

Instead, I would like to encourage you to begin focusing instead on what you ***do*** want. Our mental images and prevalent thoughts are so much more powerful than we realize, as they're literally the blueprints for our external reality. I know this may sound a bit "out there" to some of you, but even Einstein was a proponent of this theory. He believed that imagination was more important than knowledge. This was because he understood that our known reality was simply a result of what we imagined in the past. He was aware that we are continually creating a new reality, based on our thoughts.

And on a personal note, I have seen this in my own life time and time again. It's absolutely amazing what we can create when we visualize it! Just think—what if you really could create the life of your dreams without limitations?

Take a moment now and let your mind open to the possibilities. What would you wish for if you really believed you could have it? I recommend that you think in terms of your inner life as well as your outer life, as both are important for true fulfillment and happiness. Next, allow yourself to believe, even if just for a moment, that you really do have everything you desire and you're living a life of abundance and joy. Now, think about this—you can begin right now to create this life! You really and truly can have every little thing your heart desires. ***Yes!*** Isn't that exciting? All that it requires are two simple things: Believing and doing.

First, you must believe in it enough to visualize it every day. Visualize it as if it were happening in the present moment—see yourself living your ideal life and imagine how it would feel. The more you can see it, and especially feel it, the more you will become a magnet for it. Of course, along with visualizing your ideal life, you must also be willing to take steps in the direction of your dreams. But I encourage you to focus on the visualization aspect first. Allow the proper steps to present themselves to you, as they most assuredly will. You simply cannot go wrong if you're visualizing your ideals and taking steps in the direction of your ideal life. Life is meant to be lived in joy and you were given dreams for a reason! Now it's time to use the great gift of visualization to achieve these dreams. See it, feel it, and then . . . live it!

Meditation

In my experience, nothing creates a foundation of inner wellness as powerfully as meditation. It's the ultimate way to rejuvenate your whole being as well as relax and center yourself. Meditation produces deeply beautiful changes in our lives and brings us into harmony with our intuition and inner wisdom. Meditation makes us calm, focused, joyful, and clearheaded. As we meditate more and more, we transition into a state of alignment with our highest self. And by doing so, we are automatically able to share more with those around us—without even saying a word. Just by being in a higher state of consciousness, we create a beautiful ripple effect all around us.

To begin your meditation practice, it's helpful to find a place that's relaxing and free from distractions. You can start by finding a comfortable chair that is in a private (or at least quiet) location. Alternatively, you can meditate lying down if you feel confident that you can remain alert. The ideal position is one that encourages both comfort and alertness. Once you've found your happy place, you can then begin with either one of the following meditations:

Breathing Meditation: This is such a simple technique, yet so powerful! Begin by getting comfortable and relaxing your body. Next, become aware of your breath. Don't try to change the way you're breathing—just become aware of your breath as it flows in and out of your body. Once you've spent a few minutes in breath awareness, you can move on to the next step—and there are two options here. Option one is to use a visualization. To do this, imagine beautiful light flowing into your body with each inhale. See that light healing, uplifting, and charging you with positive energy. As you exhale, imagine anything you no longer wish to hold onto flowing out of you and leaving you for good.

The second option is to use affirmations. To do this, begin by thinking a positive affirmation along with each inhale. For example, you could say "I am allowing love and light to fill my being." As you exhale, let go of something using a counter affirmation. For example, you could think the following as you exhale: "I am letting go of all fears." Using this breathing method will not only relax you, it will also create powerful, positive changes before you know it. Truly!

Full Body Relaxation: This is an ideal stress reliever. Begin by getting comfortable and allowing all of your muscles to relax completely, starting with your toes. Imagine working all the way up to the top of your head, allowing any stress to melt away in each area as you go. Although many practitioners of meditation begin with the head and work their way down, this method will help you maintain a higher state of consciousness.

Once you're fully relaxed, imagine a brilliant, sparkling light. See that beautiful light filling your toes and feet completely. Next, bring that healing light slowly upward through every part of your body until you're totally saturated in that light from toe to head. Be as open as you can, and really feel the healing energies of that light in each part of your body. Send extra light and love to any part of your being that needs it and continue to be open to healing on all levels. Ahhhh.

Love Thyself!

Here's something you might not know—one of the most transformational and empowering things you can do only takes about ten seconds! Simply by taking a moment to look in the mirror daily to say "I love you" to yourself, you'll soon become aware of how powerful this practice is. The more you can do this, the more you'll shift into a natural state of self-love. And self-love is one of the most powerful ways to transform your habits. Think of how you treat people that you love—with care and nurturing, right? By simply practicing this quick exercise daily, you'll notice an automatic shift into much greater self-love and self-kindness.

However, if you initially find there's too much resistance in saying "I love myself," you may instead begin by saying "I am open to loving myself more and more." When we become willing and open, it automatically creates the space for greater love and empowerment. It may also be helpful for you to observe any internal dialogue as you look in the mirror. Are you thinking that you need to change in some way before you can become fully lovable? Be aware of those thoughts and allow them to gently transform. Remember, just because you can become more beautiful does not mean that you aren't already beautiful right now in this moment!

Cornerstone Four:
Eating a Diet Rich in Superfoods

So far we've talked about three of the cornerstones for a truly healthy lifestyle—a plant-based diet, exercise, and inner wellness. And while all of those are very important, now it's time to have some fun! This last cornerstone is all about, yes, deliciousness. This is the part where we talk about how to fuel your body with the ultimate in nourishment so you can be the ultimate you. It's also the part where I give you over 100 delectable, exciting recipes to get you started.

And this isn't just talk, my friends. These recipes truly are made with flavor in mind. As I always say, "We have taste buds for a reason!" There is no need to deprive yourself of flavor and satisfaction just because you want to eat a healthy diet. Au contraire! In truth, tasty food and great health go hand in hand. Isn't that just the most exciting thing ever? I'll answer that—yes, it is! It really, really is.

What are Superfoods? And Why Should I Care?

The term "superfood" is simply a type of food that's unusually nutrient dense. Superfoods are also usually high in antioxidants, fiber, vitamins, and minerals—plus, they help protect our bodies against all kinds of cancer and other diseases.

So, why cook with superfoods—are they really all that special? Yes, in fact, they are. They're not only the most nutritious foods on the planet, they're also delicious when prepared properly—and they don't have to be expensive. Sure, if you go out and spring for giant bags of chia seeds and maca, you'll be forking over some bucks. And yes, I personally love both of those foods and am willing to splurge on them because of their fabulousness. But most superfoods are easy to find, inexpensive, and familiar. For example, who hasn't heard of sweet potatoes, blueberries, and garlic? Most superfoods can be found at your local grocery store—or better yet, your local farmer's market.

Tess, Explain Yourself—You're Obsessed with Superfoods!

Busted! You are so on to me. I've been having a love affair with superfoods (please don't tell brown rice) for well over a decade. Nothing gets me more excited than nourishing my friends and family with foods that support their bodies and build up their immune systems. Plus, it's so easy to make superfoods taste delicious! And what could be more thrilling than eating a diet that's both incredibly vitalizing and totally delectable? Hence my obsession.

People often ask me how I develop my recipes. What's my creative process? The answer is largely related to my love for superfoods—I begin by thinking of a recipe concept, and then asking myself one simple question: "How can I make this dish as over-the-top nutritious as I possibly can, while simultaneously making it delectable?" Thus, the recipes in this book will nourish your body, please your palate, and make you glow with vibrant health!

Can You Explain the Superfoods Used in This Book?

Yes I can and I will. The following "Superstars" are all of the superfoods that have been used in this book. Of course, there are many other whole plant-based foods that are also healthy, but I'm not writing an encyclopedia here. These are the real standouts.

The Superstars!

♥ Acai: Pronounced ah-SIGH-ee, this superfood is higher in antioxidants than any other fruit or vegetable. I purchase it in frozen packets from the health food store— "Sambazon" is the brand.

♥ Almonds: The most alkalinizing of all nuts, almonds are also very high in calcium, iron, and fiber.

♥ Amaranth: This grain-like food is so nutritious that scientists actually had to come up with a separate class for it. It is, simply put, off the charts. If you can find amaranth greens, consider yourself lucky—they're great juiced or minced up in salads. Amaranth is very high in calcium, protein, and immune-boosting properties. It also builds strength and gives energy.

♥ Apple cider vinegar: According to the book *Folk Medicine* by Dr. D.C. Jarvis, this type of vinegar is basically a cure-all—and fans of apple cider vinegar will readily agree. It's useful for everything from curing sore throats to energizing your system.

♥ Asparagus: According to Ayurveda, asparagus is tri-doshic, meaning that it's beneficial for everyone. It's a fabulous immune-booster and is rich in antioxidants. It is also disturbingly delicious when roasted.

♥ Avocado: Do you need proof that life is good? Then consider the avocado—creamy, rich, and satisfying, this fruit is unusually high in fiber and potassium. It also contains a plethora of vitamins and minerals, making avocados a guilt-free splurge!

♥ Beans: By beans, I'm including anything from pinto beans to black beans to lentils—legumes, basically. I first discovered how awesome beans were when I dropped six dress sizes over a decade ago. Beans fill you up, not out, as they're uber-high in fiber and nutrition and very low in calories and fat. They're also a great source of iron and minerals. Go beans go!

♥ Beets: This root vegetable is living proof that the more vibrantly colored a food is, the more vitalizing it is. Beets are very high in iron, carotenoids, antioxidants, fiber, vitamins, and minerals. They can be peeled and grated raw into wraps and salads, or cooked.

♥ Bilberry: A kissing cousin of the awesome blueberry, bilberries are especially beneficial for eyesight. You can purchase bilberry juice or nectar in most health food stores. Oh and by the way, *yum.*

♥ Blueberries: These low-calorie berries have some of the highest antioxidant levels of any fruits and vegetables—which makes them a great way to protect our bodies from free radicals and disease. As if their deliciousness levels weren't enough to entice us!

♥ Broccoli: Like its cousin the cabbage, broccoli is exceptionally nutritious and anticarcinogenic. As with any green vegetable, broccoli is rich in chlorophyll and vitamins.

♥ Buckwheat: This strength-building grain has a longer transit time in the digestive system than any other grain, making it very filling and stabilizing. It's also very high in protein, calcium, and fiber.

♥ Cabbage: This highly versatile vegetable is especially nutrient-dense and anticarcinogenic. If you favor the darker, purple (so-called "red") variety, you'll get an extra boost of antioxidants, flavor, and fun.

♥ Cacao: This is a raw food version of cocoa. As a raw food, it's especially nutrient-dense and flavorful, as well as very high in antioxidants. I use two forms of cacao in my recipes—raw cacao powder and raw cacao nibs (these make a great substitute for chocolate chips). Both can be found in health food stores or online.

♥ Carob: Many people think of carob as a chocolate substitute, but I personally adore its unique flavor all on its own. Naturally sweet, carob is very alkalinizing, fiber-rich, and loaded with calcium. Unlike chocolate, carob has no oxalic acid or caffeine. It can be purchased in powdered form from any health food store.

♥ Carrots: These beta-carotene rich babies are intensely nutritious, alkalinizing, and vitamin-packed. But you already knew that, right?

♥ Cashews: According to *The New Whole Foods Encyclopedia* by Rebecca Wood, cashews are a "nutritive and warming food that support lung function." They're also high in minerals, protein, and heart-healthy fats. Use soaked, puréed cashews as a base for salad dressings, creamy desserts, or savory dips.

♥ Chia: Fairly new to the mainstream health food scene, chia seeds are an excellent source of omega-3s. They're also neutral in flavor and very versatile—use them in smoothies, shakes, and puddings. Favor black chia seeds for optimal nutritional impact.

♥ Chili peppers: Come to mama! Chili peppers (cayenne, tabasco, habanero, jalapeno, etc.) are a great way to build the immune system, get your energy moving, and fortify your body with vitamin C. Just make sure you wear gloves when handling them to prevent a plethora of unpleasantries!

♥ Cilantro: You either love it or you hate it—and I love, love, love it! This detoxifying herb is not only flavorful, it's also energizing, nourishing, and medicinal.

♥ Citrus zest: Have organic lemons, limes, or oranges on hand? Don't throw away those peels before you zest them! The zest not only contains delightful flavor, it's also exceptionally nutritious and antioxidant-rich. Be sure to use organic citrus though—with conventional produce, the peels aren't considered "food" by the USDA and thus can be sprayed exceptionally heavily with toxins.

♥ Coconut: This delicious food is warming, energizing, immune-boosting, and nurturing. Its fats are also mostly medium-chain fatty acids, which aren't as easily stored in the body as fat.

♥ Coconut water: Loaded with electrolytes and potassium, coconut water is a favorite amongst athletes for its ability to keep the body fueled, hydrated, and running strong. Surprisingly, coconut water is fat-free.

♥ Edamame: Exceptionally fiber-rich, this delicious food is about as natural a soy product as you can get. I like to purchase frozen organic edamame that is pre-shelled—I also find it unnecessary to cook edamame. Why not make life easy?

♥ Eggplant: Hello, delicious! Think of eggplant as the tofu of vegetables—plain, it's nothing special, but when you zing in some flavor, wow! Eggplant is low in calories, but high in potassium and fiber.

♥ Extra-virgin olive oil: Rich in vitamin E, this type of oil also supports liver and gallbladder function, as well as healthy cholesterol levels. Be sure to purchase an organic, high-quality oil whenever possible—the most healthful kind will be labeled "first cold pressing."

♥ Figs: Loaded with calcium, fiber, and iron, this delicious fruit is available dried in most health food stores.

♥ Flax: A superior source of omega-3s, flax is cleansing and very high in fiber. Flaxseeds can be purchased whole and then ground in a coffee grinder for maximum freshness. From there, add to smoothies, baked goods, and breading mixtures. For a healthy, natural egg replacer do the following: Stir 2 tablespoons ground flaxseeds with 3 tablespoons boiling water. Set aside for 5 minutes and use as a replacement for one egg.

♥ Forbidden rice: This delightful, hearty black rice is, as with anything, made more nutritious by its naturally intense color. Forbidden rice can be purchased in health food stores and used interchangeably with most other types of rice.

♥ Garlic: As if you didn't know, garlic is the bomb, nutritionally speaking. It's antibacterial, anticarcinogenic, detoxifying, and immune-boosting—not to mention the best thing since sliced bread. Ooh, garlic **on** sliced bread!

♥ Ginger: This book is really just an excuse to profess my undying love for ginger. Where do I begin? Ginger is immune-boosting, energizing, cleansing, and the perfect remedy for motion sickness. Ginger has also been shown to relieve inflammation, making it useful for athletes or those afflicted with arthritis.

♥ Greens: "Greens" is a blanket term I've used because I'm too lazy to list out the following foods individually: spinach, baby greens, arugula, romaine lettuce, chard, and beet greens. As you've probably heard, these foods are top-notch for keeping your body vitalized and healthy. They're high in fiber, chlorophyll, calcium, iron, and carotenoids. However, please note that some greens (kale, parsley, and cilantro) are so off-the-hook that they have their very own listing.

♥ Green tea: I know many people who swear by green tea for preventing colds and illnesses—and they're right. Green tea is immune-boosting, detoxifying, and exceptionally high in antioxidants. And if you're not crazy about the flavor, jazz it up with some mint.

♥ Hemp: Nutritious hemp is just about the best source of omega-3s available. An easy way to get hemp in your diet is to purchase hemp protein powder, which is also very high in fiber and chlorophyll.

♥ Hibiscus: Can I just tell you how amazing I feel anytime I consume something with hibiscus in it? I'm convinced it's magic. Purchase dried hibiscus in health food stores and use it to flavor teas and drinks.

♥ Kale: Kale = Love. It's also just about the most strengthening, immune-boosting, powerful veggie on the planet. Have you ever seen kale poking up through a patch of snow? It's unstoppable! Just like you'll be if you eat enough kale. I personally favor the curly kale varieties for kale chips and lacinato (also called dinosaur) kale for everything else.

♥ Lemon: A great way to alkalinize your system, fresh lemon can also perk up just about any dish. Lemon detoxifies the body, rebalances the system, and delivers loads of vitamin C. When a recipe calls for lemon juice, please be sure to use fresh lemons, as they make all the difference—for both flavor and health.

♥ Lime: Did you read what I wrote about lemons? Good—because limes are **almost** as powerful as lemons and have similar nutritional benefits. However, limes are so uniquely delicious that we forgive them for being slightly inferior to their yellow sisters.

♥ Maca: Butterscotchy-tasting maca root builds strength and endurance, making it the perfect food for athletes. It's perfect in shakes, raw cookies, and energy bars. Purchase raw, organic maca powder from health food stores or online.

♥ Mango: According to Ayurveda, mangoes are tri-doshic. This means that they're fabulous for every single body type. Mangoes are one of those foods that just give you that instant energy boost—perhaps because of their B vitamins, enzymes, and juicy fabulousness.

♥ Miso: Quite possibly the most immune-boosting and detoxifying food on the planet, miso is the ultimate "good soy." Whip up a batch of miso soup anytime you feel a cold coming on and you'll help to nip it in the bud. Purchase mellow white and also dark miso paste in the refrigerated section of health food stores.

♥ Nutritional yeast: Also called "nooch," this stuff has been around since the first flower children whipped up a batch of bean burgers. Nutritional yeast can be purchased either powdered (my preference) or flaked and gives a wide variety of savory foods a nutty, cheesy flavor. Purchase a brand such as "Red Star" that offers a variety that's especially high in vitamin B-12.

♥ Onions: This vegetable is anticarcinogenic, detoxifying, energizing, immune-boosting, and warming. Think of it as the less appreciated version of garlic.

♥ Parsley: This chlorophyll-rich herb is remarkably detoxifying and mineral-rich. It's my top choice for greens when I'm in the mood for a fresh veggie juice— nothing feels as nourishing and cleansing as a vibrant dose of parsley!

♥ Pineapple: Pineapple contains an enzyme called bromelain that has anti-inflammatory and anti-cancer properties. It's also very high in vitamins C and A as well as fiber—and besides, what better way to celebrate life than with a juicy, ripe pineapple? Heaven.

♥ Pomegranate: This glorious, vitalizing fruit has been shown to protect and treat against cancer. It has also been shown to be delicious.

♥ Pumpkin: I could go on and on about the vibrant, carotenoid-rich properties of pumpkins. But I won't—I'd rather just remind you that this fiber-rich superfood is delicious. Delicious, I tell you! Every fall, I purchase local organic pumpkins, slice them in half, and remove the seeds (which I roast separately). From there, the pumpkin halves cook face down in the oven until tender. Once cooled, I freeze the flesh in small containers so that I can enjoy the taste of fresh pumpkin all year round—in smoothies, breads, biscuits, muffins, and soups.

♥ Quinoa: Pronounced keen-wah, this amazing superfood has very high-quality protein, calcium, vitamins, and minerals. I personally favor the taste of the light tan variety as opposed to the red (dark) variety. However, the two can be mixed together for excellent (and fun) results.

♥ Raspberries: Exceptionally high in fiber, raspberries are also a great source of antioxidants and vitamin C. But forget about all of that—I have two words for you: Raspberry. Pie.

♥ Red rice: This heirloom grain is extremely high in nutrients, fiber, and cuteness. It can be purchased in health food stores and is often called "red jasmine rice."

♥ Sea vegetables: These treasures are exceptionally mineral-rich and nutrient-dense, and they will also give you glowing skin. Sprinkle dulse and kelp on popcorn, pop a stick of kombu in your pot of beans, and make fun sushi rolls using nori. For more information on sea veggies, please see page 37.

♥ Sesame: This seed-based food is warming, nourishing, and very useful for lowering cholesterol. Sesame is high in calcium and protein as well. I use the following sesame products: raw sesame oil, toasted sesame oil, sesame seeds, and sesame tahini.

♥ Shiitake mushrooms: These drool-worthy mushrooms are incredibly immune-boosting and detoxifying, as well as a great source of minerals and B vitamins. Purchase them frozen (I use "Woodstock Farms" brand) or fresh.

♥ Soy yogurt: As with any quality fermented food, soy yogurt is extremely beneficial for digestion and overall health. It's also energizing, rejuvenating, and cleansing. I favor "Nancy's" soy yogurt, as it's unusually fresh and made with high-quality ingredients.

♥ Sprouted grains: Whenever you sprout something, its nutritional profile pretty much explodes. So, if something is healthy before you sprout it, you can bet your sweet booty that it's going to be exponentially healthier once sprouted! There are lots of great sprouted products on the market today—you can purchase sprouted tortillas (both corn and wheat) and sprouted breads in any health food store, as well as many supermarkets.

♥ Strawberries: This mouth-watering fruit is an excellent source of vitamin C—a powerful antioxidant. Strawberries are also high in fiber, minerals, and vitamins. Not to mention the fact that they're pure happiness in the form of a berry.

♥ Sweet potatoes: Very high in carotenoid antioxidants (the thing that gives them their vibrant orange color), sweet potatoes are also rich in fiber and vitamin C. I think of sweet potatoes as the ultimate whole food, as they don't need anything else to taste delicious—you can just bake one up and savor it plain. What an easy, delicious way to get a glowing, bright complexion!

♥ Tempeh: When people ask me about "good" soy vs. "bad" soy, I tell them about tempeh. No matter what your views are on soy, once you take a peek at the nutritional profile of this superfood, there's no denying its power. Tempeh is a fermented food, making it exceptionally nutritious and beneficial for the digestive system. Plus, tempeh is extremely high in fiber, B vitamins, and protein.

♥ Turmeric: This pungent root has one of the highest-known sources of beta-carotene. Plus, it's extremely high in antioxidants and is remarkably medicinal. Use a little ground turmeric to add flavor, color, and nutrition to ethnic dishes, popcorn, and scrambled tofu.

♥ Umeboshi: Despite their salty nature, umeboshi products (pickled plums) are extremely alkalinizing. Umeboshi also helps to remove lactic acid from the body, which increases energy and immunity. In my kitchen, I use both ume plum vinegar and umeboshi plum paste.

♥ Walnuts: One of the very best sources of omega-3s, walnuts are also antioxidant-rich and high in vitamin E. Plus, they're one of those foods I can just feel in my body as soon as I consume them—they give me an instant energy uplift!

♥ Winter squash: Similar to pumpkin in nutritional value and preparation method, winter squash is warming, nourishing, and very rich in carotenoids.

Pantry Setup:
The Radiant Kitchen

Here's the part where you knock on my door and I show you around my kitchen—where there will be sun tea and raw vegan truffles, by the way. In this chapter are all of the essential items that go on my shopping list when I run out.

If you take the time to stock your kitchen using this guide, you'll greatly reduce the amount of shopping you'll have to do to make the recipes in this book. I know it seems like a lot of stuff, especially if you're new to this way of eating, but you'll be loving life once your kitchen is well stocked with healthy goodness. This will also reduce the "huh?" factor as you set out to make my recipes. It's a lot easier to tackle an unfamiliar recipe when you have the ingredients on hand!

For more information on what some of these lesser known superfoods are all about, please see the "Superstars" section on pages 24-32. Please also keep in mind that I recommend purchasing organic versions of these pantry staples— you're worth it! And remember, the more you familiarize yourself with these healthy basics, the easier and more natural it will become. You'll be working words like "kombu" and "maca" into casual conversation before you know it.

Whole Grain Flours:

If you live in an arid climate, these will store indefinitely in airtight (preferably glass) containers at room temperature. If you live in a more humid area, you can freeze (or refrigerate) what you won't be able to use up within a month or two.

- Whole wheat pastry flour—the perfect whole-grain replacement for white flour in any recipe. (You may substitute gluten-free all-purpose flour if you're on a gluten-free diet.)
- Whole wheat flour
- Buckwheat flour
- Cornmeal

Whole Grains:

Ah, the stuff o' life! These nourishing grains will usually keep for several months in airtight (preferably glass) containers at room temperature.

- Quinoa (pronounced keen-wah)
- Amaranth (tiny pearls of fabulousness)
- Rolled oats
- Rice varieties: Wild rice, long grain brown rice, red rice, and forbidden rice (it will be our little secret)
- Popcorn

Sweeteners:

Aside from the maple syrup, these will store for several months in airtight (preferably glass) containers at room temperature.

- Organic sugar (You'll find I use this very sparingly—however, this is still a better alternative to refined white sugar.)
- Pure maple syrup (this should be refrigerated)
- Liquid stevia
- Raw organic agave nectar (I've found raw blue agave to be the best kind.)

Dry Legumes:

These can usually be bought in bulk at your local health food store. They will store for several months or more in airtight (preferably glass) containers at room temperature.

- Black beans
- Pinto beans
- White beans (navy, cannellini, or great white northern)
- Red and brown lentils
- Black-eyed peas

Baking Items:

These will all store at room temperature for several months.

- Aluminum-free baking powder
- Baking soda
- Arrowroot (a healthy cornstarch substitute)
- Carob powder
- Sea salt
- Pure vanilla extract and mint extract

Liquid Seasoning Staples:

I keep these bad boys in the cupboard next to my stove—this makes for easy access while I'm stir-frying or whipping up a quick dinner.

- Organic shoyu, nama shoyu, or tamari (more details on p. 94) **Note:** if you are gluten-free, make sure your tamari is too—some brands contain wheat.
- Extra-virgin olive oil
- Coconut oil (I use non-virgin as it's neutral in flavor—you don't want everything to taste like coconut, right?)
- Toasted (dark) sesame oil
- Vinegars: apple cider vinegar, umeboshi (ume plum) vinegar, brown rice vinegar, and balsamic vinegar
- Sriracha Thai chili sauce and other hot sauces (such as tabasco or habanero)

Always on my Counter:

I feel very uncomfortable if these items aren't on my counter.

- Fresh limes and lemons
- Fresh garlic
- Ripening bananas (smoothie fodder once they're ripe enough to freeze)
- Fresh fruit

In the Freezer:

- Frozen bananas and berries (for smoothies and shakes)
- Frozen acai packets ("Sambazon" brand)
- Edamame (I purchase it pre-shelled—so convenient!)
- Sliced, frozen shiitake mushrooms ("Woodstock Farms" brand)
- Spices and flours that you won't be using up quickly

In the Fridge:

• Organic produce is the rock star of my fridge! I keep it in a highly visible, accessible spot. For me, this means the entire top shelf of the fridge. Doing this makes it easy to stay focused on emphasizing the most health-supporting food of all—vegetables. No more tossing them into the vegetable crisper where they are out of sight and out of mind!

• However, in the vegetable crisper, I do keep staple veggies such as onions, carrots, and potatoes, as they take up too much room on the top shelf. Also found here are "fragile" veggies (fresh herbs, lettuce, cilantro, etc.) that can freeze in certain refrigerators (mine).

• Seeds: sesame, sunflower, chia, and flaxseeds

• Nuts: whole almonds, walnuts, dry-roasted peanuts, and raw cashews

• Ground flax meal (ground flaxseeds)

• Nutritional yeast ("Red Star" vegetarian support formula is ideal.)

• Dark (or red) miso and mellow white miso

• Organic ketchup

• Hemp protein powder

• Mustards: dijon and yellow

• Vegan mayonnaise (I recommend "Vegenaise" reduced fat mayonnaise—made with flax and olive oils)

• Shredded vegan cheese (I recommend "Daiya" brand—this also freezes well)

• Nut butters (organic peanut butter and raw almond butter)

• Tahini

• Pure maple syrup (ah, sweet elixir of tree)

• Orange juice (the "not from concentrate" kind, as it's the closest thing to fresh-squeezed)

• Firm, water-packed tofu (preferably "Wildwood" sprouted tofu)

• Five-grain tempeh (this also freezes well)

• Organic sprouted corn tortillas

• Sprouted whole grain tortillas (I like "Alvarado Street" tortillas as they're made from sprouts and whole grains, making them soft yet hearty)

• Sprouted bread (I use the "Food For Life" Ezekiel bread as it's very nutritious—and a slice of it toasted with some almond butter is a great mini-meal on the go!)

Staples to Keep on Hand in the Cupboard:

- Organic canned beans (pinto, garbanzo, kidney, white, and black beans)
- Canned, diced organic tomatoes
- Jarred pimientos
- Raw cacao powder
- Raw cacao nibs
- Dried shiitake mushrooms
- Umeboshi plum paste
- Coconut butter
- Raw maca powder
- Pasta: buckwheat soba noodles, corn-quinoa pasta, and brown rice vermicelli
- Bean thread noodles (found in Asian markets and many grocery stores)
- Organic, high fiber breakfast cereal
- Spring roll skins (rice paper wrappers)
- Raisins, dried dates, dried figs, and dried cranberries
- Canned coconut milk (regular and lowfat)
- Sun-dried tomatoes and kalamata olives (once opened, they go in the fridge)

Sea Vegetables:

The rumors are true—I really do have a "sea veggie section" in one of my cupboards. They don't call me a food nerd for nothing! These mineral-rich goodies will keep indefinitely as long as they're in airtight packaging.

- Nori (packaged in large square sheets and available toasted or untoasted—either version is fine)
- Dulse flakes and kelp powder (both are a fantastic addition to popcorn)
- Kombu strips (I can't not add these to every pot of beans I cook!)

Herbs and Spices:

I store these in glass jars and refill them using bulk herbs and spices from the health food store. This is the cheapest, freshest, and least wasteful way to go. I keep the following on my spice rack:

Asafetida, basil, oregano, thyme, rosemary leaf, salt-free lemon-pepper, seasoned salt, sage leaf, dried (ground) turmeric, cayenne powder, red chili flakes, cumin powder, cumin seeds, ground coriander, black pepper, white pepper, black mustard seeds, onion and garlic granules,* dill weed, bay leaves, celery seed, ground cinnamon, ground mustard, smoked paprika, parsley, ground nutmeg, chili powder (a spice blend, not straight chilies), and pumpkin pie spice.

*Granulated onion and garlic (also called onion and garlic granules) taste much better than the powdered variety. However, they are often still labeled as "powdered" onion or garlic. What you are looking for is a product that has the consistency of tiny granules rather than powder. Think "tiny edible sand particles."

Radiant Recipes

Welcome to the deliciousness portion of our program. Here you'll find everything from addictive, crunchy snacks to rich, creamy desserts—all you'll ever need to feel satisfied, yet without any of the junk. So, I invite you to have fun with these recipes, as I joyfully created them with your ultimate health and happiness in mind. Bon appétit!

Radiant Recipe Codes

You're not a mind reader. Or are you? Either way, I've included this handy decoding system to help you figure out what's what in the recipe department. You'll see these codes at the bottom of the recipes, and now you can actually make sense of them with this cheat sheet. Let's get cooking!

• **Green:** "Green" means go! These recipes are based on vitalizing high-fiber whole foods and are low in fat. They're the ideal foods to emphasize in your daily diet for optimum health.

• **Blue:** "Blue" recipes may include higher-fat plant foods and/or natural sweeteners. However, they're still healthful enough to eat in moderation on a daily basis, especially if you're physically active.

• **GF:** This code means that the recipe is either already gluten-free, or that it can be made gluten-free with the suggested substitution(s).

• **SF:** For those who don't wish to consume soy products in any form, I've labeled the soy-free recipes as "SF." Keep in mind, however, that some recipes without this label may simply have tamari in them (which can easily be replaced with sea salt). Thus, if you're soy-free, it's always a good idea to look through the ingredients in a recipe, even when it isn't labeled as "SF."

• **30 minutes or under:** This very exciting code applies to recipes that take under 30 minutes. However, many other recipes without this code are still very easy to make—they may simply require soaking, marinating, or dehydrating.

• **R:** This code stands for recipes that contain only raw (living) food ingredients.

• **HR:** This new code on the block just moved into the neighborhood, so let's give it a warm welcome! When a recipe is coded as "HR" it means that it's minimally cooked and high in raw ingredients—however, it's not 100% raw.

• **F**: This indicates that a recipe will freeze well.

> ### Note:
>
> At the very bottom of each recipe, you'll find a list of "superstars" which are the superfoods from that recipe. For more information on the superstars, please see pages 24-32.

Breakfast and Beverages

Every morning, we have the opportunity to really start the day off right. We can choose to give our bodies vibrant, nourishing fuel that also happens to be totally yummy (such as the goodness in this chapter). When we do so, we set ourselves up for success. And even if you don't usually like to be set up, you might change your mind when you try the deliciousness that's about to happen.

Power Pancakes

I can now die knowing that I've achieved uber-healthy, gluten-free superfood pancake perfection. Although I do realize that's a little wordy for my tombstone.

Optional: "Kick Acai Strawberry Sauce" (p. 161)
- 2 tablespoons ground flax (flaxseed meal)
- 3 tablespoons boiling water

- ¾ cup vegan yogurt, plain or vanilla (I use "Nancy's" soy yogurt)
- 1½ cups nondairy milk
- 1 cup buckwheat flour
- 1 tablespoon *each:* chia seeds and maca powder
- 1 teaspoon baking powder
- ½ teaspoon *each:* sea salt and baking soda

- 1-2 tablespoons coconut oil

1. In a medium bowl, combine the flax and boiling water. Stir well and set aside for 5 minutes, until very gooey.

2. Whisk the yogurt into the flax mixture until well combined.

3. Next, whisk in the nondairy milk. Add the remaining ingredients (all except the coconut oil) and stir well to combine.

4. Set a large skillet over medium heat and add some of the oil. When the skillet is hot, pour the batter onto it in small circles or bunny shapes.

5. When the tops become bubbly and the bottoms are golden-browned, flip over. Once both sides are golden-browned, remove to a plate. Continue this delightful journey until all of the batter has been transformed into pancakes. Serve plain or topped with "Kick Acai Strawberry Sauce" or maple syrup.

Serves 4/GF/Green/F/30 Minutes or Under!

♥ Superstars: flax, soy yogurt, buckwheat, chia, maca, coconut

Breakfast Quinoa

Here's something to get overly excited about—a delicious yet simple breakfast dish wherein every single ingredient is a superstar! Although this is perfect for me as is, I do find that the sweetness of pomegranate juice can really vary. If yours comes out a bit too tart, just drizzle it with a little maple syrup or add a few drops of liquid stevia.

- 1 cup dry quinoa
- 2 cups pomegranate juice or nectar

- 1 cup fresh or frozen blueberries
- 1 tablespoon minced lemon zest
- 2 teaspoons fresh lemon juice
- 4 teaspoons sliced almonds

1. Place the quinoa and pomegranate juice in a medium pot with a tight fitting lid. Bring to a boil over high heat. Reduce heat to low and simmer (still covered) for 15 minutes, or until all of the liquid is absorbed. Remove from heat.

2. Stir in the blueberries, lemon zest, and lemon juice. Cover again to allow the blueberries to warm.

3. Stir again and served topped with almonds.

Serves 3/GF/SF/Green/F
30 Minutes or Under!

♥ Superstars: quinoa, pomegranate, blueberries, citrus zest, lemon, almonds

Chia Power Pudding

This is the simplest thing ever, yet so nourishing and vitalizing. Think of this as a basic recipe that you can play with, using other fruits and juices. I like to keep a little of this on hand (refrigerated in a glass jar) so that I can just grab a few bites when I need a boost. Works great—especially when I'm on the go!

- 1 cup pomegranate juice
- 3 tablespoons chia seeds
- ½ cup blueberries, fresh or frozen

1. Combine the pomegranate juice with the chia seeds in a small bowl. Stir and set aside for about an hour, until the pudding has thickened.

2. Stir the blueberries into the pudding and set aside for another 5 minutes or so. Stir and serve. This will keep, refrigerated in an airtight container, for up to a week.

Serves 2
GF/SF/Green/HR

♥ Superstars: pomegranate, chia, blueberries

Sweet and Savory Breakfast Fritters

These whole-food fritters aren't just for breakfast—they also work well as a light entrée, hearty side dish, or sandwich filling.

- 1 cup cooked sweet potato flesh (well mashed or blended)
- ½ cup dry quinoa
- 1 cup water
- ½ cup finely minced onion
- 1 tablespoon ground flaxseeds (flaxseed meal)
- 2 teaspoons *each:* dried ground sage and dried rosemary
- ½ teaspoon *each:* sea salt and ground black pepper
- 4 large cloves garlic, minced or pressed
- *For pan-frying:* a little non-virgin coconut oil (or olive oil)

1. Place the quinoa and water in a medium pot set to medium-high heat. Cover and bring to a boil. Reduce heat to low and simmer until the quinoa is tender and all of the water is absorbed, about 15-20 minutes. Remove from heat.

2. In a medium bowl, stir the sweet potato together with the quinoa. Stir in the remaining ingredients (except for the oil) until thoroughly combined.

3. Set a medium-large skillet over medium-high heat and add a little oil. Form the mixture into thin, 2-inch wide patties and place on the skillet, leaving room in between each fritter. Fry until the undersides are browned, about 2-3 minutes. Flip over and cook the other side until golden-browned, another 2-3 minutes. Remove to a plate. Repeat this process until all of the mixture has been used up. Serve immediately.

Serves 4/GF/SF/Green/F

♥ Superstars: sweet potatoes, quinoa, onion, flax, garlic, coconut

> Having cooked, cold sweet potatoes on hand at all times is the bomb! One of my favorite meals in a pinch is simply a cooked, cold sweet potato that's been sliced and pan-fried in a teaspoon of coconut oil, with or without a sprinkle of rosemary. So simple, so good!

 Frozen Bananas

This is more of a technique than a recipe, but I've heard too many disturbing stories about poor banana freezing methods to leave it out! I like to use very ripe bananas for this purpose. I find that I can always omit added sweeteners from my smoothies and shakes because a really ripe banana lends the perfect amount of sweetness.

Ingredient: Bananas (ripe or very ripe)

1. Peel the bananas and discard the peels (not onto the floor).

2. Break into 1 or 2-inch pieces and place in a plastic bag. Leave enough room (don't overpack the bag) so that the chunks can freeze individually. Seal the bag so that it is airtight.

3. Place in the freezer, laying the bag flat, so that the pieces can spread out and won't freeze together too much. After they have been frozen for 8-10 hours, they will be ready to use. They will keep for several weeks or longer in the freezer. If, at some point they do freeze together, simply thump the bag on the counter with feigned rage. They will separate out of fear.

Serves: the purpose
GF/SF/Green/R/F

Dark Chocolate Raspberry Shake

Just in case you forgot how much you're loved.

- One frozen banana (p. 46)
- 1 cup "Sweet Almond Milk" (p. 56) or other nondairy milk
- 1 cup frozen raspberries
- 3 tablespoons *each:* raw cacao powder and raw agave nectar
- 1 tablespoon raw maca powder
- 1 teaspoon vanilla

Blend all of the ingredients until thoroughly emulsified. A blender is very handy for the aforementioned task. Serve immediately and feel the love!

Serves 2
GF/SF/Blue/R/F
30 Minutes or Under!

♥ Superstars: almonds, raspberries, cacao, maca

Eye Love You Smoothie

Want to simultaneously support your eye health and taste a blueberry explosion? It's as simple as whipping up a batch of this. Both blueberries and bilberries protect the eyes while supporting digestion and immunity. And don't get me started on their antioxidant levels.

- 1½ cups bilberry nectar (or blueberry nectar)
- 1 frozen banana (p. 46)
- 1 cup frozen blueberries

Optional: 1 tablespoon chia seeds

Place all of the ingredients in a blender and blend until smooth and thoroughly combined. Serve immediately.

Serves 2
GF/SF/Green/R/F
30 Minutes or Under!

♥ Superstars: bilberry, blueberries, chia

Spicy Pumpkin Pie Shake

Part dessert, part breakfast, this shake will give your skin a glow and your brain a boost.

- 2 frozen bananas (p. 46)
- 1¼ cups cooked pumpkin, very cold
- 1 cup cold "Sweet Almond Milk" (p. 56) or other nondairy milk
- 3 tablespoons maple syrup, cold
- 1 tablespoon pumpkin pie spice
- ½ teaspoon vanilla

In a blender, combine all of the ingredients until thoroughly smooth and emulsified. Serve immediately, you pumpkin lover you.

Serves 2
GF/SF/Blue/HR/F
30 Minutes or Under!

♥ Superstars: pumpkin, almonds

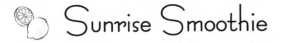 # Sunrise Smoothie

This thoroughly refreshing smoothie is a surefire way to start the day off feeling great! Plus, it's a banana-free alternative for those times when you just aren't into monkey business.

- 1 cup frozen raspberries
- 1 cup mango chunks, fresh or frozen
- 1½ cups pineapple juice

Blend all of the ingredients well in a blender and serve. Happiness!

Serves 2/GF/SF/Green/R/F
30 Minutes or Under!

♥ Superstars: raspberries, mango, pineapple

Strawberry Vanilla Milkshake

- 2 cups frozen strawberries
- 1 banana, fresh or frozen (p. 46)
- 1 cup nondairy milk
- 1 tablespoon *each:* chia seeds, raw maca powder, vanilla, and maple syrup

Blend all of the ingredients well and enjoy pure vegan milkshake bliss!

**Serves 2/GF/SF (if using soy-free milk)/Green/HR/F
30 Minutes or Under!**

♥ Superstars: strawberries, chia, maca

Blueberry Bliss Smoothie

Just four ingredients—each one chosen for its amazing health benefits and flavor compatibility. By the way, I want to marry this particular smoothie.

- 1 cup frozen blueberries
- ¾ cup plain soy yogurt (I use "Nancy's" brand)
- ½ cup pomegranate juice
- 1 tablespoon chia seeds

Blend all of the ingredients well and serve immediately. Didn't I tell you? Yep, marriage material for sure.

Serves 1/GF/Green/HR/F/30 Minutes or Under!

♥ Superstars: blueberries, soy yogurt, pomegranate, chia

🍋 Acai The Light Smoothie

Chocolate and acai are a match made in heaven—who woulda guessed? Acai (pronounced ah-sigh-EE) is insanely high in antioxidants, boasting 10 times the amount of red grapes. In fact, every item in this smoothie will supercharge your health and leave you glowing, energized, and feeling fantastic.

- 1 3.5 oz. packet frozen acai purée (I use "Sambazon" brand)
- 1 banana, frozen (p. 46)
- 2 tablespoons raw cacao powder
- 1 tablespoon *each:* raw maca powder, hemp protein powder, chia seeds, and maple syrup
- 1 cup "Sweet Almond Milk" (p. 56) or other nondairy milk

1. Run the acai packet under hot water until you're able to break it into pieces through the plastic using your fingers. Which is really quite fun if you stop and think about it.

2. Place the acai and all other ingredients in a blender and blend until smooth. If necessary, add a little more almond milk until the desired consistency is reached. Drink up and feel the love.

Serves 1
GF/SF/Green/R/F
30 Minutes or Under!

♥ Superstars: acai, cacao, maca, hemp, chia, almonds

Maca My Day

Mmmaca. It's like healthy butterscotch that makes you want to do power lifts and climb peaks. You know, that sort of thing.

- One frozen banana (p. 46)
- 1 tablespoon maca powder
- 1 tablespoon ground flaxseed meal
- 1 teaspoon vanilla extract
- ¾ cup "Sweet Almond Milk" (p. 56) or other nondairy milk

Place all of the ingredients in a blender. I'll bet you know what comes next. Yeah, hit the "on" button and watch the magic unfold. Drink up and feel amazing!

Serves 1
GF/SF/Green/R (if using raw almond milk)/F
30 Minutes or Under!

♥ Superstars: maca, flax, almonds

 # Lemon-Lime Aid

This drink will aid you greatly in alkalinizing your body, staying hydrated, detoxifying, and just enjoying life in general. I recommend drinking at least one serving of this every day for glowing health.

- 2 cups pure water
- ¼ cup fresh lemon juice
- 3 tablespoons fresh lime juice
- ¼ teaspoon liquid stevia

Mix all of the ingredients together and stir. Serve plain or over ice.

Serves 1
GF/SF/Green/R/F
30 Minutes or Under!

♥ Superstars: lemon, lime

Pineapple Hibiscus Cooler

This drink has it all—coconut water for electrolytes, green tea for antioxidants, hibiscus and lime for vitamin C and body alkalinity, and pineapple for enzymes and yumminess. Drink up and feel beautiful! Well, more beautiful, that is. You're already gorgeous, baby.

- 2 green tea teabags
- 2 tablespoons dried hibiscus, placed in a tea strainer
- 2 cups boiling water
- 5 cups pineapple juice, the fresher the better
- 1½ cups coconut water (approximately the amount from one young Thai coconut)
- ¼ cup plus 2 tablespoons fresh lime juice

1. Pour the boiling water over the teabags and hibiscus and let steep for 15 minutes. Discard the teabags and hibiscus.

2. Pour the tea into a large pitcher and stir in the remaining ingredients. Serve at room temperature or chilled.

Makes about 9 servings/GF/SF/Green/HR/F
30 Minutes or Under!

♥ Superstars: green tea, hibiscus, pineapple, coconut water, lime

Sweet Almond Milk

This is a lighter, sweeter almond milk than the version in **Radiant Health, Inner Wealth**. However, feel free to omit the stevia if you prefer a more all-purpose beverage. Happy milking!

- ¾ cup raw almonds
- 4 cups water
- ¼ teaspoon sea salt
- ⅛ teaspoon liquid stevia

1. Place the almonds in a blender and cover with a little of the water (just enough to blend). Blend until as smooth as possible. Add the remaining water, sea salt, and stevia. Blend well. Say "blend" some more.

2. Place a fine meshed strainer over a wide mouth container. Pour the almond milk over the strainer and into the container in small batches, cleaning the strainer and removing the almond meal as needed. Discard the almond meal, or save for cookies or body scrub—or anything else your sweet little heart desires.

3. Transfer the strained milk to a glass quart jar and refrigerate. This will keep for about a week.

Makes one quart of almond milk
GF/SF/Blue/R
30 Minutes or Under!

♥ Superstar: almonds

Sauces and Dressings

Here are the recipes that will make your food life extra saucy and delicious. Keeping a few of these babies on hand at all times will make it easy to whip up a yummy, healthy meal in no time—and to entice picky eaters to try things they might not otherwise. Enjoy!

Miso Healthy Dressing

This tangy dressing will jazz up any salad, veggie pasta toss, tempeh, or grain dish. Miso is incredibly immune-boosting and detoxifying, so you can feel great about indulging in this incredibly tasty dressing!

- ¼ cup *each:* raw cashews, balsamic vinegar, and sesame oil (raw, not toasted)
- ½ cup *each:* water and chopped onion
- 2 tablespoons dark miso (I use red miso)
- 1 tablespoon tamari

1. In a blender or food processor, blend the cashews, vinegar, and oil until smooth.

2. Add the remaining ingredients and blend until very smooth and no lumps remain. This will keep, refrigerated in an airtight container, for several weeks.

Makes 1¾ cups dressing (14 servings)
GF/Green/HR
30 Minutes or Under!

♥ Superstars: cashews, sesame, onion, miso

Guilt-Free Ranch Dressing

Never thought you'd see the day? Welcome . . . it's bright and sunny here. With a 100% chance of delicious ranch dressing that you'd never guess was healthy and vegan! Oh, and by the way, every kid (omnivorous or vegan) I've tested this on has loved it—and had no idea it was any different than store-bought ranch dressing!

- 1 cup reduced fat "Vegenaise" vegan mayo (made with olive and flax oils)
- 2 tablespoons water
- 4 teaspoons apple cider vinegar
- 4 teaspoons minced fresh parsley (or dried parsley)
- 4 small-medium cloves garlic, pressed or minced
- 1 teaspoon onion granules
- ½ teaspoon sea salt

Place all of the ingredients in a tightly covered jar and shake well until thoroughly combined. This will keep, refrigerated in an airtight container, for a week or more. Use as a dip for fresh vegetables, a dressing for salads, or as a bath.

Makes about 6 servings
GF/Blue
30 Minutes or Under!

♥ Superstars: flax, apple cider vinegar, parsley, garlic

 # Maple Mustard Dressing

This flavorful dressing is perfection on the "Asparagus Walnut Sunshine Salad" (p. 118). It's also great drizzled over greens (cooked or raw), roasted vegetables, or steamed Brussels sprouts.

- 3 tablespoons prepared yellow mustard
- 2 tablespoons maple syrup
- 1 tablespoon *each:* water and extra-virgin olive oil
- 1 teaspoon *each:* tamari and apple cider vinegar

Stir or shake all of the ingredients together. This will store, refrigerated in an airtight container, for several weeks.

Makes about ½ cup dressing (4 servings)
GF/Green
30 Minutes or Under!

 ♥ Superstars: turmeric (mustard), extra-virgin olive oil, apple cider vinegar

Lemon Ginger Miso Dressing

Yes, I'm obsessed with the combination of lemon, ginger, and miso. And no, I will not stop.

- ½ cup raw cashews, soaked for several hours or overnight
- ½ cup water
- ¼ cup fresh lemon juice
- 2½ tablespoons *each:* chopped fresh ginger and chopped white onion
- 2 tablespoons mellow white miso
- Dash of tamari, or to taste

Blend all of the ingredients together until smooth. Serve over salads, Asian noodles, or steamed vegetables. This will keep, refrigerated in an airtight container, for at least a week.

Makes about 1½ cups dressing (8-12 servings)
GF/Green/R
30 Minutes or Under! (needs soaked cashews)

♥ Superstars: cashews, lemon, ginger, onion, miso

Ume Sesame Dressing

I love this dressing very deeply for four reasons: One—it's the yum. Two—it's lowfat. Three—it's totally healthy. Four—it takes 30 seconds to make.

- 2 teaspoons brown rice vinegar
- 1 teaspoon *each:* umeboshi (ume plum) vinegar and toasted sesame oil

Stir ingredients together and pour over 4 cups of salad. Sorry to complicate your life so much—can you ever forgive me?

Serves 1/GF/SF/Green/30 Minutes (seconds, actually) or Under!

♥ Superstars: umeboshi, sesame

Ginger Soy Dipping Sauce

This simple, cleansing sauce is perfect for spring rolls, summer rolls, potstickers, dumplings, and Asian noodle or vegetable dishes. Best of all, it comes together in under 5 minutes!

- ¼ cup tamari or shoyu
- 2 tablespoons *each:* brown rice vinegar and grated fresh ginger
- 1 teaspoon toasted sesame oil
- ½ teaspoon red chili flakes

Stir all of the ingredients together and serve. This will keep, refrigerated in an airtight container, for at least a week.

Makes ½ cup of sauce (8 servings)/GF/Green/30 Minutes or Under!

♥ Superstars: ginger, sesame, chili peppers

Onion Dill Miso Dressing

This delicious, tangy dressing is perfect over salads, grains, roasted veggies, or poured directly into your mouth. Let's do this thing.

- ¼ cup chopped onion, white or yellow
- ¼ cup extra-virgin olive oil
- 2 tablespoons apple cider vinegar
- 1 tablespoon *each:* tamari and mellow white miso
- 1 teaspoon dried dill

Place all of the ingredients in a blender and process until smooth. This will store, refrigerated in an airtight container, for at least a week—unless, of course, you decide to take a bath in it, as one of my recipe testers suggested.

Serves 4
GF/Blue/HR
30 Minutes or Under!

♥ Superstars: onion, extra-virgin olive oil, apple cider vinegar, miso

Everyday Chicky Gravy

Why everyday? Because this is so low in fat and high in nutrients that you can slather it on everything (yes, **everything**) and feel guilt-free about it! Plus it's easy peasy oh so pleasy to whip together. Pour it over mashed or baked potatoes, tofu or tempeh cutlets, grains, or use in the "Happiness Bowl" (p. 140-141).

- 1 tablespoon coconut oil (not extra-virgin)
- 2 cups sliced shiitake mushrooms
- Medium white or yellow onion, sliced (1½ cups sliced onion)

- 15 oz. can white beans, rinsed and drained
- 1¾ cups water
- ¼ cup plus 2 tablespoons "Chicky Baby Seasoning" (p. 67)
- ¼ cup nutritional yeast powder
- 2 tablespoons balsamic vinegar
- 1 tablespoon *each:* tamari and olive oil (or melted non-virgin coconut oil)
- 5 large cloves garlic, peeled
- 1 teaspoon sea salt

1. Set a medium skillet or wok over medium-high heat. Add the 1 tablespoon of coconut oil, along with the mushrooms and onions. Sauté for about 10 minutes, stirring often, until the mushrooms and onions are lightly browned.

2. Transfer to a blender and add the remaining ingredients. Blend until smooth.

3. Before serving, warm gently in a pan. This will keep for about a week, refrigerated in an airtight container.

Makes about 5 cups of gravy (10 servings)
GF/Green/F/30 Minutes or Under!

♥ Superstars: coconut, shiitake mushrooms, onions, beans, nutritional yeast, garlic

Sweet 'N Sour Sauce

This may be the healthiest sweet and sour sauce known to humans. Of course, flamingos and wild dogs have known about it for centuries. Serve this versatile sauce over stir-fried veggies, crusted tempeh or tofu, or grains.

- 2 cups *each:* water and pineapple chunks, fresh or frozen
- 3.5 oz. packet of plain frozen acai ("Sambazon" brand)
- 1 cup chopped onion, white or yellow
- ½ cup apple cider vinegar
- ⅓ cup raw agave nectar
- ¼ cup *each:* arrowroot powder and coconut oil
- 2 tablespoons *each:* chopped fresh ginger and natural ketchup
- 4-5 large cloves garlic, peeled
- 1 teaspoon sea salt

1. Place all of the ingredients in a blender and process until completely smooth.

2. Place in a pan set to medium heat. The mixture will begin to thicken (due to the arrowroot) once it gets hot. Whisk (using a wire whisk) frequently until the sauce is thick and warm. Serve immediately or store, refrigerated in an airtight container, for a week or more.

Makes about 5 cups of sauce
GF/SF/Green
30 Minutes or Under!

♥ Superstars: pineapple, acai, onion, apple cider vinegar, ginger, garlic

 Pretty Pico

This is a very healthy and colorful twist on pico de gallo (the fresh, raw salsa found in many Mexican restaurants). Serve with organic, baked tortilla chips or on fajitas, burritos, tostadas, or tacos.

- 2½ cups diced fresh tomatoes (use a mix of red, orange, and yellow if possible)
- ½ cup *each:* finely diced white onion, chopped cilantro, and finely diced cucumber
- ¼ cup *each:* grated carrot, minced jalapeno, and fresh lime juice
- 2 large cloves garlic, minced or pressed
- 1 teaspoon sea salt

Place all of the ingredients in a medium-large bowl and stir gently until well combined. Store in an airtight container, refrigerated, for several days.

Makes about 4 cups (serves 8)
GF/SF/Green/R
30 Minutes or Under!

 Superstars: onion, cilantro, carrots, chili peppers (jalapeno), lime, garlic

Chicky Baby Seasoning

I've surrendered to the fact that this recipe just cannot stay out of any of my cookbooks. It has become a favorite with so many of my readers and works great in a plethora of recipes. I stopped buying expensive, clumpy, pre-made vegetarian chicken seasonings when I realized how easy it was to make my own. I also love how healthy this version is, as it's totally free from suspicious ingredients and chock full of B vitamins from the nutritional yeast.

- 1 cup nutritional yeast powder
- 3 tablespoons *each:* dried onion granules and seasoned salt
- 2 teaspoons *each:* celery seed and dried garlic granules
- 2 tablespoons dried parsley flakes
- 1 teaspoon *each:* lemon-pepper, organic sugar, dried dill, and dried rosemary
- ½ teaspoon *each:* ground black pepper and white pepper

Place all of the ingredients in a container with a tight fitting lid. Shake very well until thoroughly combined. Store at room temperature out of direct sunlight. This will keep for several months.

Makes about 1½ cups of seasoning mix
GF/SF/Green/F
30 minutes or under!

♥ Superstars: nutritional yeast, garlic, parsley

Snacks and Dips

Oh yes, snacks and dips. The stuff food fantasies and parties are made of! Here's the coolest twist ever, though—these delectable treats are actually power-packed with nutrients and goodness. So, picture this: You're vegging out, watching your favorite movie, and getting your snack on. But there is zero guilt for once, because you're eating something that's not only delicious but also totally nourishing. How exciting is that?!

Sweet 'N Spicy Turmeric Popcorn

I knew the title of this recipe was spot-on when my daughter tried this and said: "Hmmm . . . it's sweet, then it's spicy. It's sweet **and** spicy. Plus, it has turmeric." This addictive snack is yet another fun way to sneak the powerhouse magic of turmeric and cayenne into your bod!

- 1 tablespoon non-virgin coconut oil
- ¼ cup popcorn kernels
- 1 tablespoon raw agave nectar
- ½ teaspoon ground turmeric
- ¼ teaspoon *each:* sea salt and ground cayenne

1. Set a medium pot with a tight fitting lid over medium-high heat.

2. Add the oil. Once it melts, add the popcorn. Cover and pop, shaking often, until the time in between pops slows to about 2-3 seconds. Remove from heat.

3. Drizzle with the agave and sprinkle with the turmeric, salt, and cayenne. Stir well to mix, then serve. And yes, your yellow fingers will return to normal at some point in the near future.

Serves 1-2
GF/SF/Green
30 Minutes or Under!

♥ Superstars: coconut, turmeric, chili peppers

Zesty Lemon Kale Chips

Lemon + Lemon Zest + Kale = Best. Thing. Ever.

- 4 cups (lightly packed) kale, de-stemmed and torn into 2-inch pieces
- 3 tablespoons fresh lemon juice
- 1 tablespoon extra-virgin olive oil
- ½ tablespoon minced lemon zest (zest of one large lemon)
- ¼ teaspoon sea salt

1. In a large bowl, combine all of the ingredients thoroughly.

2. Spread out in a single layer on dehydrator trays, giving the kale pieces space (don't overlap). Dry on low heat (105° - 115° F) until all of the pieces are crunchy and dried. This will take about 7-12 hours.

3. Place the chips in an airtight jar and store for a week or more.

Serves 2
GF/SF/Green/R

♥ Superstars: kale, lemon, extra-virgin olive oil

 # Babaganoush

If I had only known years ago how easy it is to make delicious babaganoush! Things would have been different, that's for sure. I credit Kathy Keyes from the Pagosa Baking Company for the inspiration—the secret is to squeeze out all of the water after the eggplant is baked. Serve this with "Sprouted Dipper Chips," (p. 73), pita wedges, crackers, raw veggies, or whole grain artisan bread.

- One medium eggplant
- ¼ cup plus 2 tablespoons fresh lemon juice
- ¼ cup *each:* tahini and extra-virgin olive oil
- 4 large cloves garlic, peeled
- 1 teaspoon sea salt
  Optional garnishes: Chopped parsley, smoked paprika, kalamata olives, and extra-virgin olive oil

1. Preheat your oven to 400° F.

2. Cut the eggplant in half lengthwise. Place it cut side down on a lightly oiled cookie sheet and bake for 40 minutes, or until the eggplant is very tender. Set aside to cool.

3. Once cool, squeeze all of the moisture out of the eggplant by wringing it with your hands. This is pretty much a party at your sink, if you stop and think about it. You should end up with 2 cups of eggplant. Place the eggplant (skin and all) in a food processer and blend well.

4. Add the remaining ingredients (all but the garnishes) and blend until as smooth as possible. There will still be some seeds, so smooth is a relative term here! Just make sure no chunks of garlic, etc., remain. Serve cold or at room temperature, with or without the optional garnishes. This will keep, refrigerated in an airtight container, for up to a week.

Makes about 2½ cups dip (5 servings)/GF/SF/Blue

♥ Superstars: eggplant, lemon, sesame, extra-virgin olive oil, garlic

 # Sprouted Dipper Chips

These simple, wholesome wedges are perfect for dipping in the "Babaganoush" (p. 72) or "Supercharged Hummus" (p. 78). For fun and prizes, feel free to spice these up by sprinkling the tops with zatar, sesame seeds, garlic, minced onion, and/or dried herbs of your choice.

- 3 sprouted whole grain tortillas (such as "Food For Life" or "Alvarado Street")
- 2 teaspoons oil (olive or melted non-virgin coconut) for brushing

1. Preheat the oven to 375° F.

2. Cut each tortilla into 8 wedges (like a pizza). Place the pieces on baking sheets in a single layer.

3. Brush each piece very lightly with the oil and bake for about 10 minutes, or until lightly browned and crisp. Please note that not all of the pieces will brown at the same rate. Be prepared to single out the early achievers. Serve the chips warm or at room temperature. Once cooled, they can be stored in an airtight container for a few days.

Serves 6
SF/Green/F/30 Minutes or Under!

♥ Superstar: sprouted grains (tortillas)

Spicy Moroccan Sweet Potato Fries

Mmmoroccan. Sweet and savory, Moroccan flavors are perfect with just about anything—especially sweet potatoes. Serve these yummy baked "fries" as a side dish, snack, or light entrée.

- 1 medium sweet potato, cut into French fry shapes (2½ cups)
- 2 teaspoons *each:* melted coconut oil and fresh lime juice
- 1½ teaspoons organic sugar
- ¾ teaspoon *each:* cinnamon and ground cumin
- ¼ teaspoon *each:* paprika and sea salt
- ⅛ teaspoon *each:* garlic granules and ground cayenne

Optional: lime wedges (for serving)

1. Preheat your oven to 400° F. In a medium bowl, combine all of the ingredients (except for the optional lime wedges). Toss or stir until the potatoes are coated evenly with the seasonings.

2. Spread the potatoes out on a large baking sheet, making sure that the pieces don't overlap. Bake for 10 minutes.

3. Remove from the oven and flip the "fries" over. Bake for another 10 minutes, or until browned and tender. Serve immediately. If desired, serve with the lime wedges for looks and personality.

Serves 1-2
GF/SF/Green
30 Minutes or Under!

♥ Superstars: sweet potato, coconut, lime, garlic, chili peppers (cayenne)

Rawcho Cheese Dip

This dip is my latest obsession—I even dream about it. You've been warned.

- ½ cup raw cashews
- 4 oz. jar pimientos, drained
- ¼ cup nutritional yeast powder
- 3 tablespoons fresh lemon juice
- 3 medium-large cloves garlic, peeled
- 2 tablespoons water
- 1 teaspoon granulated onion
- ¾ teaspoon sea salt
- ¼ teaspoon ground cayenne

Blend all of the ingredients in a food processor (or good blender) until completely smooth. Serve cold or at room temperature with raw vegetables, baked tortilla chips, or raw crackers. This will store, refrigerated in an airtight container, for at least a week.

Makes about 1 cup of dip (4 servings)
GF/SF/Blue/R
30 Minutes or Under!

♥ Superstars: cashews, nutritional yeast, lemon, garlic, chili peppers (cayenne)

 # Bold Lime Kale Krunchers

These addictive chips are incredibly healthy and ridiculously fun to eat. As I happen to love lime to death, I was very heavy handed with the lime flavor here. However, if you're a mild child, cut the lime juice in half. (p.s. I just ate a whole batch of these for breakfast. And I don't even regret it.)

- 4 cups (lightly packed) kale, washed well and drained
- 3 tablespoons fresh lime juice
- 2 tablespoons sesame oil (raw, not toasted)
- 1 tablespoon sesame seeds
- ¾ teaspoon sea salt (or less if you prefer)

1. Tear the kale into 2-inch pieces, removing the thick stems.

2. In a large bowl, toss the kale with the remaining ingredients and mix very well.

3. Place on food dehydrator trays in a single layer (don't overlap the pieces). "Cook" at low heat (105° – 115° F) for 7-12 hours, or until crunchy and fully dehydrated. Once completely cooled, store in an airtight container at room temperature for a week or more.

Serves 4 (unless one of them is me)
GF/SF/Green/R

 Superstars: kale, lime, sesame

Green Velvet Guacamole

Here's a lower fat, full-flavor guacamole that will rock your socks. Serve with organic tortilla chips or crudités (raw veggies), or as a topping for anything and everything Mexican.

- Flesh of 2 medium avocados
- 1 cup shelled edamame (thawed if frozen)
- 5 tablespoons fresh lime juice
- 3 large cloves garlic, peeled
- 1 teaspoon sea salt

In a food processor or blender, emulsify all of the ingredients until silky smooth. This will store, refrigerated in an airtight container, for several days.

Makes 8-10 servings/GF/Green/R
30 Minutes or Under!

♥ Superstars: avocado, edamame, lime, garlic

Supercharged Hummus

OK, I gotta admit it—I am *so* crazy excited about this recipe! Take a regular, delicious hummus and supercharge it with incredibly uber-nourishing ingredients? Oh yeah! Let's make this party happen.

- 15 oz. can chickpeas, rinsed and drained (1½ cups chickpeas)
- ½ cup fresh lemon juice
- ¼ cup tahini
- 2 tablespoons *each:* nutritional yeast, mellow white miso, water, and extra-virgin olive oil
- 1 tablespoon umeboshi plum paste
- 2 large cloves garlic, peeled

Blend all of the ingredients until fully emulsified. Personally, I find a food processor best fits the bill for this task. Remove to an airtight container and store in the fridge for up to one week. This is delicious served with raw veggies, "Sprouted Dipper Chips" (p. 73), or whole grain crackers. It's also great with fresh veggies and sliced avocado in wraps or sandwiches.

Makes about 2 cups of hummus (8 servings)
GF/Green/F/30 Minutes or Under!

♥ Superstars: beans, lemon, sesame (tahini), nutritional yeast, miso, extra-virgin olive oil, umeboshi, garlic

 # Zippy Dippy

Yes indeed, this is one zippy doo dah of a bean dip. However, the bold flavors also make for bold health—fresh lemon and lots of garlic ensure that you'll have a spring in your step and an immune system that's made of iron!

Bean dip:
- 15 oz. can pinto beans, rinsed and drained (about 1½ cups beans)
- ¼ cup fresh lemon juice
- 2 tablespoons extra-virgin olive oil
- 3 large cloves fresh garlic
- ¾ teaspoon sea salt

Optional Topping:
- ½ cup "R.O.C.K. The Top" (p. 130) or ¼ cup chopped parsley

For dipping, use any or all of the following:
- "Sprouted Dipper Chips" (p. 73)
- Baked blue corn tortilla chips (such as "Guiltless Gourmet")
- Raw vegetables (carrots, red pepper strips, celery, cauliflower, etc.)

1. In a food processor or blender, combine the bean dip ingredients until completely smooth and silky.

2. Transfer to a bowl and sprinkle with the optional topping, if using. Serve with chips and/or veggies. This dip will keep for about a week, refrigerated in an airtight container.

Serves 4-6/GF/SF/Green
30 Minutes or Under!

♥ Superstars (for just the dip): beans, lemon, garlic, extra-virgin olive oil

Vegan Cheese Sticks

Yeah, I know—this stretches the boundaries of what a superfood recipe "should" be. But we all need a little comfort food now and then, right? So, we might as well make it as healthy as possible, while still keeping deliciousness as a priority!

Cheesy Filling:
- ¾ cup cauliflower purée (steam cauliflower until tender and blend until silky smooth)
- 1½ cups grated vegan cheese (I use "Daiya" mozzarella)

Crunchy Breading:
- 1¼ cup fine bread crumbs (pulse sprouted grain bread in a food processor)
- 2 tablespoons chia seeds (or ground flaxseeds)
- 2 teaspoons dried parsley
- 1 teaspoon dried basil
- ½ teaspoon *each:* sea salt and garlic granules

For pan-frying: 2-3 tablespoons coconut oil (not extra-virgin)
For serving: "Guilt-Free Ranch Dressing" (p. 59) or vegan marinara sauce

1. Stir the filling ingredients together and set aside.

2. In a large bowl, combine the breading ingredients thoroughly and set aside.

3. Now I'm about to tell you something very honest, but I trust you can handle it: This next step is going to be tricky. In fact, you might wonder if you can do it. At one point, you may even curse me and my "fricking stupid recipe." But I promise that if you hang in there, you'll not only get the hang of it, but also be in a very comfortable position—one that involves gooey, scrumptious cheese sticks.

4. Are you ready to get on board? Then roll up your sleeves and roll up the cheese. To do the latter, remove about 2 tablespoons of cheesy filling and roll it into a little log formation. Next, roll it in the breading until thoroughly coated on all sides. Place on a plate. Repeat until all of the filling is used up, placing all of the sticks on a plate (leaving enough room so that they don't touch each other). Pop the plate in the freezer for 25 minutes.

5. Heat a large skillet over medium-high heat and add the oil. Remove the plate from the freezer. Once the oil is hot, place the cheese sticks on the pan in a single layer and cook, uncovered, until the bottoms are golden-browned. Turn over and continue to cook until golden-browned on all sides. This will take about 2 minutes on each of the 4 sides, for a total of 8 minutes.

6. Remove to a plate and serve either plain or with one of the sauces.

Makes 12 vegan cheese sticks (serves 3-4)/Blue/F

♥ Superstars: sprouted grains, chia, parsley

Raw Cinnamon Rolls

Think of these as a quick, delicious, healthy alternative to packaged energy bars. Since they're so nutrient-dense, just one little roll can be surprisingly satisfying!

- 1 cup raw walnuts
- ½ cup raisins
- ½ cup (packed) pitted dates (about 12 dates)
- 2 teaspoons cinnamon
- ¼ teaspoon *each:* sea salt and ground nutmeg

1. Place all of the ingredients in a food processor. Blend until well combined and very crumbly, but don't over-blend—you want to retain some texture.

2. Pull out small pieces of the mixture and roll into 1-inch balls with your hands. These will store in an airtight container, refrigerated, for several weeks or more.

Makes 18 rolls (9 servings)/GF/SF/Green/R/F/30 Minutes or Under!

♥ Superstar: walnuts

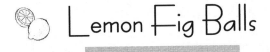# Lemon Fig Balls

Welcome to perfection on a hiking trail.

- ½ cup *each:* raw almonds, raisins, and raw walnuts
- 6 dried figs (about ½ cup, packed), stems removed
- ¼ cup fresh lemon juice
- 4 teaspoons (packed) lemon zest
- ¼ teaspoon sea salt

1. Place all of the ingredients in a food processor. Blend until well combined and very crumbly, but don't over-blend—you want to retain some of the fun texture.

2. Pull out small pieces of the mixture and roll into 1-inch balls with your hands. These will store in an airtight container, refrigerated, for several weeks or more.

Makes 18 rolls (9 servings)
GF/SF/Green/R/F
30 Minutes or Under!

♥ Superstars: almonds, walnuts, figs, lemon, citrus zest

Gingersnap Nuggets

Simple, quick, nuggety, and yummy—don't think I don't know what excites you.

- 1 cup *each:* raw walnuts and raisins
- 1 tablespoon ground ginger
- ¼ teaspoon *each:* sea salt and ground nutmeg

1. Place all of the ingredients in a food processor. Blend until well combined and very crumbly, but don't over-blend—you want to retain some of the texture.

2. Pull out small pieces of the mixture and roll into 1-inch balls with your hands. These will store in an airtight container, refrigerated, for several weeks or more.

Makes 18 rolls (9 servings)
GF/SF/Green/R/F
30 Minutes or Under!

♥ Superstar: walnuts

Sides and Starters

Looking for something to brighten up your day and/or life? These delicious dishes will do just that! Many of them even double as easy entrées. Enjoy!

Roasted Rosemary Butternut Squash

Think of this as the Clark Kent of superfood dishes. No one would guess that it has the superpowers—in fact, it's so seemingly normal that you can serve it to your 85-year-old Aunt Edna without even one raised eyebrow.

- 1 medium butternut squash, peeled, seeded and cut into 1-inch cubes (9 cups cubed squash)
- 3 tablespoons oil (olive or melted non-virgin coconut)
- 2 tablespoons maple syrup
- 1 tablespoon finely minced rosemary (fresh or dried)
- ¾ teaspoon sea salt
- ¼ teaspoon black pepper

1. Preheat the oven to 425° F.

2. In a large bowl, toss the cubed squash with the remaining ingredients until well combined. Spread out in a single layer on a large baking sheet.

3. Bake for 30 minutes and then gently turn over. Bake for another 15 minutes, or until the squash is very tender and browned in places. Serve immediately.

Serves 4/GF/SF/Green/F

♥ Superstar: winter squash

Power Potatoes

If you have cooked potatoes on hand, this mouth-watering side dish will come together in under 15 minutes. It boasts seven different superfoods, so you can feel great about devouring this insanely yummy dish!

- 1 tablespoon coconut oil
- 3 large cloves garlic, peeled and thinly sliced
- 1 teaspoon sesame seeds, preferably black

- 2 medium potatoes (baked and cooled), chopped (2 cups chopped potatoes)
- ½ teaspoon ground turmeric
- ⅛ teaspoon ground cayenne

- 2 scallions, trimmed and chopped into 1-inch pieces
- ½ teaspoon plus ⅛ teaspoon sea salt
- 2 tablespoons fresh lime juice

1. In a large skillet or wok, heat the coconut oil over medium-high heat. Add the garlic and sesame seeds and stir-fry for 2 minutes, or just until the garlic begins to brown.

2. Add the potatoes and sprinkle evenly with the turmeric and cayenne. Stir gently to combine the ingredients well. Stir-fry until the potatoes are lightly browned, about 3-5 minutes.

3. Add the scallions and sprinkle evenly with the salt. Stir-fry for one minute. Sprinkle with the lime juice, stir well, and serve.

Serves 2/GF/SF/Green
30 Minutes or Under! (requires cooked potatoes)

♥ Superstars: coconut, garlic, sesame, turmeric, chili peppers (cayenne), onions (scallions), lime

🍋 Umeboshi Rice

This unusual, healthy, and delicious dish will soothe your stomach and cleanse your body—not to mention make you want a second bowl!

- 1 cup brown rice (short or long grain)
- 2 cups water

- 1 tablespoon umeboshi (ume plum) vinegar
- 1 tablespoon fresh lime juice
- 1 teaspoon umeboshi plum paste
- 2 tablespoons oil (raw sesame, non-virgin olive, or melted non-virgin coconut)
- 1 teaspoon brown rice vinegar

Add last:
- ½ cup minced scallions (about 3 green onions, trimmed and minced)
- ¼ cup *each:* minced carrots and finely chopped red cabbage

1. Place the rice and water in a medium pot with a tight-fitting lid. Bring to a boil over high heat, then reduce heat to low and simmer until all of the water is absorbed and the rice is tender. Set aside to cool.

2. In a large bowl, combine all of the remaining ingredients (aside from the scallions, carrots, and cabbage). Stir well until smooth. Add the cooled rice and stir to combine well.

3. Stir in the vegetables and serve. Leftovers will keep refrigerated in an airtight container for several days. However, don't reheat this dish as that will mess with its juju—serve it cold or at room temperature for optimum good karma.

Serves 4/GF/SF/Green

♥ Superstars: umeboshi, lime, onions (scallions), carrots, cabbage

Lovely Lemon Spaghetti Squash

This dish was a big hit at a cooking class I taught last fall—what a fresh, delightful way to use the nutritious (and always fun!) spaghetti squash.

- 2 medium spaghetti squash (you will need 4 cups cooked squash)

Lemon Caper Sauce:
- 4 tablespoons *each:* extra-virgin olive oil, fresh lemon juice, kalamata olives, and minced fresh parsley
- 8 medium cloves garlic, pressed or minced
- 2 teaspoons capers
- ½ teaspoon *each:* sea salt and ground black pepper

Green Garnish:
- ¼ cup fresh chives, chopped

1. Preheat the oven to 400° F. Cut the spaghetti squash in half and scoop out the seeds. Set the seeds aside—or they can be tossed with seasoned salt and oil, then baked until browned.

2. Place the squash halves face down on a baking sheet. Add about ¼-inch water to the pan. Bake until a fork proves the flesh very tender, about 50 minutes.

3. Meanwhile, place the sauce ingredients in a large bowl and stir. Set aside.

4. When the squash is tender, use a fork (or flattery) to coax the strands out. Add 4 cups of the flesh to the sauce and stir well to mix. Serve warm, topped with fresh chives.

Serves 4/GF/SF/Green

♥ Superstars: winter squash, extra-virgin olive oil, lemon, parsley, garlic

Rustic Rebel Risotto

This quick and healthy alternative to traditional risotto (made with refined Arborio rice) is truly delicious—sometimes a little rebellion can be a good thing!

- 1½ cups short grain brown rice
- 4 cups plain, unsweetened nondairy milk (preferably almond)
- ¼ cup "Chicky Baby Seasoning" (p. 67)
- 2 cups sliced shiitake mushroom caps
- 2 tablespoons fresh garlic, minced or pressed (about 16 cloves)
- 3 tablespoons extra-virgin olive oil
- 1 teaspoon black pepper

- 2 tablespoons minced fresh rosemary
- 1¼ teaspoons sea salt

Optional Garnishes:
- 2 tablespoons roasted pine nuts (dry toast in a pan just until lightly browned)
- 4-6 rosemary sprigs

1. Place all of the ingredients (except for the rosemary, salt, and optional garnishes) in a covered pot. Bring to a boil over high heat. Stir.

2. Reduce heat to low and simmer (keeping the lid on), stirring occasionally, until the liquid has been almost completely absorbed and the rice is al dente.

3. Stir in the rosemary and salt and serve. If desired, garnish with the pine nuts and rosemary sprigs.

Serves 4-6
GF/SF/Blue/F

♥ Superstars: shiitake mushrooms, garlic, extra-virgin olive oil

Fast and Forbidden Fried Rice

If you have cooked rice on hand, this dish will come together in a lickety smack. And for all you cuteness junkies out there, you'll be happy to know that it's extremely colorful too, due to the brilliant and nutrient-rich ingredients.

- 1 cup forbidden rice (black rice)
- 2 cups water

- 2 tablespoons sesame seeds
- 1 tablespoon each: non-virgin coconut oil and toasted sesame oil

- 2 tablespoons tamari
- ¾ cup scallions (trimmed and cut into ½-inch pieces on the diagonal)
- Medium carrot, diced
- ½ cup shelled edamame
- 1 tablespoon minced fresh ginger

- 2 large cloves garlic, pressed

1. Place the rice and water in a covered pot and bring to a boil over high heat. Reduce heat to low and simmer until the rice is tender and all of the water has been absorbed. Let the rice cool in the fridge for at least an hour (to prevent mushy fried rice).

2. In a wok or large skillet, heat the sesame seeds and oils over medium-high heat. Stir well and cook for one minute.

3. Add the tamari, scallions, carrot, edamame, ginger, and cooled rice and stir well to combine. Cook for 2-3 minutes, stirring often. Stir in the garlic until well combined. Say "stir" a few more times. Remove from heat and serve.

Serves 4/GF/Green/F

♥ Superstars: forbidden rice, sesame, carrots, edamame, ginger, garlic

Fresh Summer Rolls

What could possibly be better than crunchy, healthy, yummy summer rolls? Wait, don't answer that. It's irrelevant.

- "Ginger Soy Dipping Sauce" (p. 62)

Sesame Tofu Sticks:
- 7 oz. extra-firm tofu (use sprouted tofu if possible)
- 1 tablespoon tamari or shoyu
- ½ teaspoon garlic granules
- 2 tablespoons sesame seeds
- 2 teaspoons non-virgin coconut or sesame oil

- 2 oz. brown rice noodles (vermicelli) or bean thread noodles
- 1 cup *each:* shelled edamame (thawed if frozen), grated carrots, chopped cilantro, and shredded cabbage
- 12 spring roll skins (rice paper wrappers)

1. Prepare the sauce and set aside.

2. Cut the tofu into 4 slabs and gently press out any excess water using paper towels. Cut each slab into thirds vertically to form a total of 12 tofu sticks. Place on a plate and sprinkle evenly with the tamari, garlic, and sesame seeds. Set a medium skillet to medium-high heat and add the oil. Place the tofu sticks on the skillet in a single layer and cook for 3-5 minutes, or until the undersides are golden-browned. Flip over and cook the other side in the same way. Remove from heat and set aside.

3. Cook the rice noodles according to the directions on their package. Drain and set aside.

4. Prepare all of the veggies and set them aside. Feel free to get all cute with this. In my world, this means lots of little dishes--one for each filling.

5. Fill a large bowl or pan with warm water. Gently immerse a spring roll wrapper in the water and let it become soft. Don't oversoak the wrapper, however, as it can become weak if you do so. Remove from the water, letting the excess moisture drip off, and lay on a flat, clean surface.

6. Place a tofu stick, some noodles, and a little of each vegetable in the center of the wrapper. Next, fold the sides in, keeping parallel edges. Roll the bottom up and over the filling. Finally, continue to roll all of the way up. Good job! I knew you could do it. Now, do this 11 more times or until all of your fillings are used up. Serve with the "Ginger Soy Dipping Sauce."

Makes 12 summer rolls (serves 6)
GF/Green/HR
30 Minutes or Under!

♥ Superstars: ginger, chili peppers, sesame, edamame, carrots, cilantro, cabbage

Miso Sesame Edamame

Holy freaking superfood explosion! Hope you can handle it. Serve this as a starter or side dish for Asian meals or as a filling for wraps or summer rolls.

- 10 oz. bag frozen shelled edamame (1¾ cups), thawed

Saucy Sauce:
- 1 tablespoon sesame seeds, preferably black
- 1½ teaspoons *each:* toasted sesame oil, raw agave nectar, and umeboshi (ume plum) vinegar
- 1 teaspoon mellow white miso
- 1 teaspoon orange juice
- ½ teaspoon tamari
- 2 large cloves garlic, pressed or minced

Combine all of the sauce ingredients (everything but the edamame) in a medium bowl. Stir until thoroughly combined and lump-free. Stir in the edamame and serve cold or at room temperature. If you have any superhero tasks on your to-do list, now would be a good time.

Serves 4/GF/Green
30 Minutes or Under!

♥ Superstars: edamame, sesame, umeboshi, miso, garlic

> *A note about tamari:*
> When my recipes call for tamari, you can use either tamari, shoyu, organic soy sauce, or nama shoyu. If you're gluten-free, be sure to check the label of whatever kind of sauce you buy—many are made with wheat.

🍋 Ben's Veggie Pack

Have you ever had one of those dinners—you know, the kind that you could never, ever forget? Mine happened after an afternoon spent harvesting veggies from my friend Ben's garden. We dug up baby carrots and red potatoes, then snipped fresh kale and rosemary—this simple, yet divine, dish was the result.

- 2 cups very thinly sliced red potatoes (about 2 medium potatoes)
- 1 cup kale, de-stemmed and cut into thin ribbons
- ½ cup thinly sliced carrots
- 8 large cloves garlic, peeled and quartered
- 1 tablespoon extra-virgin olive oil
- 1 teaspoon dried rosemary
- ½ teaspoon *each:* sea salt and ground pepper

1. Preheat your oven to 400° F.

2. Combine all of the ingredients in a large bowl and toss or stir well until thoroughly mixed. Place in a large baking dish and cover.

3. Bake for 15 minutes, then remove from the oven. Stir well, cover, and place back in the oven. Bake for another 10-20 minutes, or until all of the vegetables are very tender and nicely browned in spots. Serve immediately.

Serves 2
GF/SF/Green/F

♥ Superstars: kale, carrots, garlic, extra-virgin olive oil

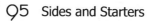

Hint:
This dish also works well as a camping recipe—hence the words "veggie pack" in the title! Simply place all of the ingredients in foil and cook over your fire.

Fresh Shiitake Sesame Spring Rolls

Fresh, crunchy, vitalizing, and totally satisfying. Yep, that's literally how we roll up in these here parts! Bring it.

- 10 oz. sliced shiitake mushroom caps (about 1½ cups)
- 2 teaspoons *each:* toasted sesame oil, sesame seeds, and tamari
- 3 large cloves garlic, minced or pressed

- 1 cup *each:* chopped cilantro, shredded cabbage, and grated carrots
- ½ cup *each:* chopped fresh basil leaves and dry-roasted peanuts (crushed)
- 4 scallions, trimmed and cut into eight 3-inch segments

- 8 spring roll skins (rice paper wrappers)
- 3 tablespoons toasted sesame seeds (toasted in a dry skillet just until lightly browned)
- Thai sweet red chili sauce (available in most grocery stores and Asian markets)

Optional: Sriracha sauce

1. In a skillet or wok, stir-fry the shiitakes, toasted sesame oil, sesame seeds, and tamari over medium-high heat. Stir often and cook until all of the liquids have been absorbed. Stir in the garlic and remove from heat.

2. Prepare all of the remaining ingredients and set aside, preferably in individual dishes—if you're into maximum organization and cuteness, that is.

3. In a large plate or bowl, soak a spring roll wrapper in warm water for under a minute (just until it become pliable and soft). Gently remove and place on a clean surface.

4. Place some shiitakes, cilantro, cabbage, carrots, basil, peanuts and a scallion segment in the center of the wrap. Don't overfill, though, tempting as it may be.

5. Next, fold the sides in, keeping parallel edges. Roll the bottom up and over the filling. Finally, continue to roll all of the way up—what you're going for here is a spring roll shaped object.

6. Sprinkle the top with sesame seeds and repeat steps 3, 4, and 5 until you have eight little cuties. Serve with Thai sweet red chili sauce (and Sriracha sauce if you want some extra heat).

Makes 8 spring rolls
GF/Green/HR
30 Minutes or Under!

♥ Superstars: shiitake mushrooms, sesame, garlic, cilantro, cabbage, carrots, onions (scallions), chili peppers

Soups and Sammies

Ah, soups and sandwiches . . . the stuff lunches (and life) are made of. The following dishes are the ultimate in comfort food—not only are they healthy, but they will also fill up your belly with delectable happiness! And who doesn't want that? Nobody—and especially not someone as smart as you.

Holy Shiitake Lentil Soup

The perfect answer to a rainy day, this delicious soup will lift your spirits, nourish your body, and make your house smell like pure happiness.

- 1 cup brown lentils
- 5 cups water
- 1 cup (packed) sliced shiitake mushroom caps
- ¼ cup "Chicky Baby Seasoning" (p. 67)

- 1 cup finely chopped kale, stems removed
- 2 tablespoons balsamic vinegar
- 1 tablespoon *each:* dried rosemary and extra-virgin olive oil
- 5 large cloves garlic, minced or pressed
- 1½ teaspoons sea salt

1. Place the lentils, water, shiitakes, and "Chicky Baby Seasoning" in a large pot or pressure cooker. Cover and bring to a boil over high heat. Reduce heat to low and simmer until the lentils are very tender. This will take about 45 minutes in a regular pot or 20 minutes in a pressure cooker.

2. Remove from heat and immediately stir in the remaining ingredients. Once the kale is wilted, serve. This will keep, refrigerated in an airtight container, for a week or so.

Serves 4
GF/SF/Green/F

♥ Superstars: beans (lentils), shiitake mushrooms, kale, extra-virgin olive oil, garlic

Simple Sesame Miso Soup

Here's a 5 minute soup that will nourish you like crazy. Eat this anytime you need an immune boost, as the miso and garlic will work wonders to eliminate toxins from your body and keep you vibrant and healthy.

- 3 tablespoons red miso
- 2 cups water
- 1 cup shelled edamame
- 1 tablespoon toasted sesame seeds
- 1 teaspoon toasted sesame oil
- 4 medium cloves garlic, minced or pressed

1. In a medium pot, whisk the miso with ¼ cup of the water in order to form a smooth paste.

2. Add the remaining water and edamame to the pot and warm over low heat. Don't ever allow the miso to boil, as it can lose its beneficial nutrients if overheated.

3. Once warmed through, stir in the remaining ingredients and remove from heat. Serve.

Serves 3/GF/Green
30 Minutes or Under!

♥ Superstars: miso, edamame, sesame, garlic

Ginger Lime Carrot Soup

This soup is pure, vibrant, delicious health in a bowl! If it were any healthier, it might be illegal in certain states. In fact, let's just keep this between you and me.

- One medium sweet potato, baked until soft (1 cup sweet potato flesh)

- 3 medium-large carrots, trimmed and chopped (1½ cups chopped carrots)
- 2 cups plus 1 additional cup nondairy milk (plain and unsweetened)

- 2 tablespoons grated fresh ginger
- 1 tablespoon fresh lime juice
- 2 large cloves garlic, minced or pressed
- 1¼ teaspoons sea salt
- ¼ - ½ teaspoon ground cayenne (½ teaspoon will make it very spicy)
For serving: ¼ cup chopped cilantro

1. Bake the sweet potato if you haven't already done so. Remove the skin and set aside.

2. In a medium pot, place the carrots in 2 cups of the nondairy milk. Cover and bring to a boil over medium-high heat. Reduce heat to low and simmer, uncovered, until the carrots are tender. This should take about 20 minutes.

3. Place the sweet potato in a blender along with the carrots and milk. Add the additional 1 cup of milk and all of the remaining ingredients (except the cilantro). Blend well, until very smooth. Serve immediately, topped with cilantro. Let the moaning begin!

Serves 4/GF/SF (if using soy-free milk)/Green

♥ Superstars: sweet potatoes, carrots, ginger, garlic, lime, chili peppers (cayenne)

15 Minute White Bean and Kale Soup

This soup comes together in a flash and promises to deeply nourish you with every single ingredient. The perfect solution to a long and stressful day!

- Two 15 oz. cans white beans (northern or cannelini), drained and rinsed
- 1 cup lightly packed kale
- 1 cup nondairy milk (plain and unsweetened)

- ¼ cup fresh lemon juice
- 1 tablespoon extra-virgin olive oil
- 3-4 large cloves garlic, pressed or minced
- 1 teaspoon *each:* black pepper, sea salt, dried dill, celery seed, and balsamic vinegar

1. In a blender, combine the beans, kale, and milk until smooth. Transfer to a soup pot.

2. Warm the mixture over medium-low heat. Add the remaining ingredients and stir well. As soon as the mixture is warmed through, remove from heat and serve. This will keep, refrigerated in an airtight container, for about a week.

Serves 3
GF/SF (if using soy-free milk)/Green/F
30 Minutes or Under!

♥ Superstars: beans, kale, lemon, extra-virgin olive oil, garlic

Thai Coconut Treasures Soup

Sweet, savory, nourishing, and soothing. Hope you can live with that.

First:
- 14 oz. can coconut milk
- 3 cups filtered water
- ½ cup dried shiitake mushrooms
- ½ cup finely chopped onion, yellow or white
- ¼ cup *each:* organic sugar, tamari, and chopped fresh basil
- 2 tablespoons grated ginger (or galangal root)

Optional:
- 2 kaffir lime leaves and a lemongrass stalk

Last:
- 3 tablespoons fresh lime juice
- 2 scallions, trimmed and chopped
- Medium tomato, chopped

1. Place the "First" (and "Optional," if using) ingredients in a medium soup pot and bring to a boil over high heat. Reduce heat to low. Simmer for 10 minutes and remove from heat.

2. Stir in the "Last" ingredients and remove the lime leaves and lemongrass (if you used them—if you didn't use them, forget I ever mentioned this). Serve hot or warm.

Makes 6-8 servings/GF/Blue
30 minutes or under!

♥ Superstars: coconut, shiitake mushrooms, onions, ginger, lime

Rockin' Red Tempeh Wrap

Tempeh wraps + love = the stuff of life.

- 8 oz. tempeh, cut into ½-inch cubes
- ½ cup water

- 1 tablespoon non-virgin coconut oil
- 3 tablespoons tamari
- 3½ tablespoons fresh lemon juice
- 1 tablespoon smoked paprika
- ¼ teaspoon ground cayenne
- 5 large cloves garlic, minced or pressed

- 2-3 sprouted grain tortillas, warmed if desired

Fixins (to taste):
- Dill pickles, chopped lettuce, and thinly sliced onions
- Vegan mayonnaise (I use "Vegenaise" brand reduced fat mayo)
- Dijon mustard

1. In a large skillet or wok, heat the tempeh and water over medium-high heat. Cover and let steam until the water is evaporated, about 3-5 minutes.

2. Add the oil, tamari, lemon juice, smoked paprika, and cayenne to the pan and stir well (but gently) to evenly coat the tempeh. Stir-fry for about 5 minutes, or until the tempeh is browned and hot. Remove from heat and stir in the garlic.

3. *To assemble the wraps:* Place the tempeh and fixins in the middle of your tortillas and roll up. Enjoy!

Makes 2-3 wraps/Green/30 Minutes or Under!

♥ Superstars: tempeh, coconut, lemon, chili peppers (cayenne), garlic, sprouted grains (tortillas), onions

Crunchy Tempeh Fajitas

Talk about your superstar lineup! These yummy, ridiculously healthy fajitas will have you feeling like a superhero in no time. Yes, they do take a bit of work (about an hour of prep time for all of the items), but they're worth it. Plus, you'll have some fun things (guacamole, pico, and "R.O.C.K." topping) left over to jazz up your burritos and tacos for the rest of the week. At least, that's the way I play it! Good times.

Tempeh Part One:
- 8 oz. tempeh, cut into ten strips
- 2 tablespoons *each:* tamari and lime juice
- 5 medium cloves garlic, pressed or minced

- "Green Velvet Guacamole" (p. 77)
- "Pretty Pico" (p. 66)
- "R.O.C.K. The Top" (p. 130)

Tempeh Part Two:
- ¼ cup plus 2 tablespoons cornmeal
- 3 tablespoons whole amaranth (uncooked)
- 1 tablespoon salt-free chili powder
- ¾ teaspoon sea salt

Optional heat: ⅛ teaspoon ground cayenne
For pan-frying: 3 tablespoons non-virgin coconut oil

Veggie Mix:
- 1 teaspoon non-virgin coconut oil
- One red bell pepper, seeded and sliced in thin strips
- 1 cup sliced shiitake mushroom caps
- 2 teaspoons tamari
- ½ cup thinly sliced kale
- 2 large cloves fresh garlic, pressed or minced

Wrap It Up Already: 4 sprouted grain tortillas

1. Place the tempeh strips on a large plate and cover with the 2 tablespoons of tamari and lime juice, as well as the 5 cloves of garlic. Set aside.

2. Make the guacamole, pico, and "R.O.C.K." topping. Set aside.

3. Place the tempeh coating ingredients (cornmeal, amaranth, chili powder, salt, and cayenne) in a plastic bag and shake well to mix. Place the tempeh strips in the bag, two at a time, and shake gently to coat. Preheat a large skillet to medium-high heat and add the 3 tablespoons of oil. Once it melts, place the coated tempeh strips on the pan in a single layer. Cook, turning occasionally, until the tempeh is browned on all sides. This should take about 5-7 minutes.

4. Meanwhile, in a medium skillet, heat the 1 teaspoon of oil over medium heat and add the red bell pepper, shiitake mushrooms, and tamari. Stir-fry until the vegetables are crisp-tender, about 5 minutes. Stir in the kale and garlic and heat for about 1 minute, until the kale is bright green. Remove from heat and set aside.

5. Warm the tortillas in a dry skillet. To assemble your masterpieces, place some tempeh, veggie mix, guacamole, pico, and topping along the center of each tortilla. Roll up and serve immediately.

Serves 4/Green

♥ Superstars: tempeh, amaranth, garlic, coconut, shiitake mushrooms, sprouted grains (tortillas), lime, avocado, edamame, chili peppers, kale, cilantro, onions

Chicky Chickadillas

These little cuties are a snap to whip up and make for such a satisfying lunch or dinner!

- 15 oz. can chickpeas, rinsed and drained (1½ cups chickpeas)
- ½ cup grated carrots
- 2 tablespoons "Chicky Baby Seasoning" (p. 67)
- 4 large cloves garlic, minced or pressed
- 1 tablespoon fresh lime juice
- ¼ teaspoon sea salt

- 1 teaspoon non-virgin coconut oil
- 2 large whole grain tortillas, preferably sprouted
- ⅔ cup grated vegan cheese (I use "Daiya" brand—either flavor works well)

- ½ cup thinly sliced onion, white or yellow
- ½ cup baby greens

Optional, for serving: fresh salsa, "Pretty Pico" (p. 66), and/or "Green Velvet Guacamole" (p. 77)

1. Place the drained chickpeas in a medium bowl. With a potato masher (or other tool of your choice), mash the chickpeas. You don't want them completely smooshed though—be sure to leave plenty of chunks in there for texture.

2. Add the carrots, "Chicky Baby Seasoning," garlic, lime juice, and salt to the chickpeas and stir well to combine. Set aside.

3. Heat a large skillet over medium heat and add the coconut oil. Once the oil is melted, place a tortilla in the skillet. Top the tortilla evenly with the chickpea mixture and sprinkle the cheese on top. Cover with the remaining tortilla.

4. Cover the pan and cook for about 4 minutes, until the bottom tortilla is lightly browned. Gently flip the whole thing over and cook an additional 4 minutes, until both sides are nicely browned. Remove to a plate.

5. Gently remove the top tortilla and place the onions and greens inside, on top of the melted cheese. Place the tortilla back on top and cut the chickadilla into 8 wedges. Serve immediately, either plain or topped with salsa, "Pretty Pico," and/or "Green Velvet Guacamole."

Serves 2-4
SF/Blue
30 Minutes or Under!

♥ Superstars: beans (chickpeas), carrots, garlic, lime, coconut, sprouted grains (tortillas), onions, greens

BBQ Chickadillas

The wild west cousin of Chicky Chickadillas, this bad boy of an entrée is quick, easy, and really satisfying.

- 15 oz. can chickpeas, rinsed and drained (1½ cups chickpeas)
- ½ cup grated carrots
- ½ cup natural, vegan barbeque sauce
- 4 large cloves garlic, minced or pressed

Optional: 1 teaspoon smoked paprika

- 1 teaspoon non-virgin coconut oil
- 2 large whole grain tortillas, preferably sprouted

- ½ cup thinly sliced onion, white or yellow
- ½ cup baby greens
- ¼ cup vegan mayonnaise (I use "Vegenaise" reduced fat)

To taste: dill pickles, sliced

1. Place the drained chickpeas in a medium bowl. With a potato masher (or other appropriate tool), mash the chickpeas. You don't want them too smooth though—having some chunky texture adds to the fun.

2. Add the carrots, barbeque sauce, garlic, and paprika to the chickpeas and stir well to combine. Set aside.

3. Heat a large skillet over medium heat and add the coconut oil. Once the oil is melted, place a tortilla in the skillet. Top the tortilla evenly with the chickpea mixture and cover with the remaining tortilla.

4. Cover the pan and cook for about 4 minutes, until the bottom tortilla is lightly browned. Gently flip the whole thing over and cook an additional 4 minutes, until both sides are nicely browned. Remove to a plate.

5. Carefully remove the top tortilla and place the onions, greens, vegan mayo, and pickles inside.

6. Place the tortilla back on top and cut the chickadilla into 8 wedges. Serve immediately to your adoring fans.

Serves 2-4
Blue
30 Minutes or Under!

♥ Superstars: beans (chickpeas), carrots, garlic, coconut, sprouted grains (tortillas), onions, greens

Grilled Cheese Greatness

This sandwich is pure awesomeness—not only delicious, it's also quite possibly the healthiest grilled cheese currently on the planet. Leave it to my mad scientist brain to make a grilled cheese into something your body will love! Hope you dig it.

- 2 slices sprouted grain bread (I use "Food For Life" Ezekiel bread)
- 2 teaspoons mellow white miso
- 1 large clove of fresh garlic, pressed
- ¼ cup shredded vegan cheddar cheese (I use "Daiya" brand)
- 1 teaspoon non-virgin coconut oil

1. Spread one slice of bread evenly with the miso and garlic. Next, add the cheese and top with the remaining slice of bread.

2. Preheat a skillet to medium heat.

3. Spread the outside of the bread with the coconut oil and place the sandwich on the heated skillet. Cook, covered, for 3-4 minutes on each side (or until the outsides are golden-browned and the inside is gooey paradise). Serve.

Serves 1
Blue/30 Minutes or Under!

♥ Superstars: sprouted grains (bread), miso, garlic, coconut

Sexy Salads and Vibrant Veggies

It's no mistake that the words "sexy" and "vibrant" are used here. Fresh vegetables are the ideal food for looking and feeling your absolute finest—and that's not just talk! I've found that nothing does more for my overall health than the simple act of eating lots of organic, fiber-rich vegetables every day. But don't believe me—try it for yourself! If you eat at least six cups of fresh vegetables each day for two weeks, I guarantee you'll notice all kinds of wonderful benefits. Viva those veggies!

Uptown Salad

Inspired by the fun, creative salad at Uptown Kitchen in Granger, Indiana, this fresh dish is more like an entrée. I know it looks complicated, but if you have cooked rice on hand, this food party will happen in no time!

Garlic Tofu:
- 7 oz. firm or extra-firm tofu (use sprouted tofu if available)
- 4 teaspoons tamari
- 2 teaspoons non-virgin coconut oil, divided
- 8 large cloves garlic, peeled and sliced

Cilantro Rice:
- 2¼ cups cooked brown rice
- 3 tablespoons minced cilantro
- 1½ tablespoons fresh lime juice
- 3 medium cloves garlic
- ¼ plus ⅛ teaspoon sea salt

Spicy Mango Salsa:
- 2 mangoes, peeled and cut into small cubes (2½ cups diced mango)
- ½ cup minced cilantro
- 2 tablespoons *each:* minced onion and fresh lime juice
- 2 teaspoons agave nectar or maple syrup
- 1 teaspoon red chili flakes
- ¾ teaspoon sea salt

Bean There, Done That:
- 15 oz can black beans, rinsed and drained

Veggie Freshness:
- 2 cups baby greens or baby spinach
- 1 cup *each:* grated carrots and shredded purple cabbage
- Small avocado, peeled and sliced or cubed

1. Slice the tofu into ½-inch thick slabs and press with paper towels to remove excess moisture. Cut into ½-inch cubes. Sprinkle evenly with the tamari and set aside.

2. Next, prepare the rice by stirring all of the "Cilantro Rice" ingredients together. Set aside. Prepare the salsa in the same way and set it aside as well. Next, prepare your beans and veggies so that everything will be ready to go when the tofu is done.

3. In a skillet or wok, heat 1 teaspoon of the coconut oil over medium-high heat. Add the garlic and stir-fry until lightly golden-browned. Remove to a plate.

4. In the same skillet, add the other teaspoon of oil and the tofu cubes. Stir-fry gently until golden-browned. Remove from heat and toss with the garlic.

5. *To get this party started:* Place some of the baby greens (or spinach) in bowls. Top with beans, rice, carrots, and cabbage. Add the garlic tofu. Top with the avocado and mango salsa. Serve immediately.

Serves 3
GF/Green/HR
30 Minutes or Under! (needs cooked rice)

♥ Superstars: coconut, garlic, cilantro, lime, mango, onions, chili peppers, beans, greens, carrots, cabbage, avocado

Springtime Celebration Salad

What would spring be without asparagus and strawberries? Actually, never mind—I don't want to know.

- 3 cups asparagus, trimmed and chopped into 1-inch pieces
- 3 cups mixed baby greens
- 1 cup sliced strawberries
- ½ cup very thinly sliced onion, white or yellow
- 1 tablespoon *each:* balsamic vinegar and raw agave nectar
- 2 teaspoons *each:* extra-virgin olive oil, tamari, and sesame seeds (preferably black)
- 1 teaspoon fresh lemon juice

1. Steam the asparagus for 5 minutes, or until bright green and crisp-tender. Remove from heat and set aside.

2. Meanwhile, place all of the remaining ingredients in a medium bowl and toss gently until well combined.

3. Add the asparagus to the bowl. Stir and serve.

Serves 2-4/GF/Green/HR
30 Minutes or Under!

♥ Superstars: asparagus, greens, strawberries, onions, extra-virgin olive oil, sesame, lemon

Perfect Tabouli

Unlike many tabouli salads that tend to be on the bland side, this one has flavor for days. Plus, with all of the detoxifying, vitalizing, alkalinizing ingredients, this delicious salad will make you look like a movie star—and a photoshopped one at that!

- 1 cup bulgur wheat
- 1½ cups water

- ¾ cup diced cucumber
- 3 cups minced fresh curly parsley
- ¼ cup minced fresh mint
- ½ cup minced onion, white or yellow
- ¼ cup plus 2 tablespoons fresh lemon juice
- 2 tablespoons extra-virgin olive oil
- ¾ teaspoon sea salt

1. Bring the bulgur and water to a boil in a covered pot, then remove from heat. Allow to sit, covered tightly, until all of the water is absorbed and the bulgur is tender (about an hour). Fluff with a fork and set aside to cool, uncovered.

2. Stir all of the remaining ingredients together in a large bowl. Add the bulgur and stir well to mix. Viola! The perfect tabouli has now become your immediate present-moment reality. Be here; chow.

Serves about 4/SF/Green

♥ Superstars: parsley, onion, lemon, extra-virgin olive oil

Asparagus Walnut Sunshine Salad

Ay deliciousness! Unless your taste buds were tragically ruined in a fast food altercation, you are sure to love this. And by the way—this *is* health in a bowl. Don't say I never did anything nice for you.

- One batch "Maple Mustard Dressing" (p. 60)

- 4 cups asparagus, trimmed and chopped into 2-inch pieces
- 9 cups baby greens
- ½ cup thinly sliced onion, white or yellow
- 6 tablespoons raw walnut pieces

1. Prepare the dressing and set it aside.

2. Steam the asparagus for 3-5 minutes, or until bright green and crisp-tender. Remove from heat and set aside.

3. Meanwhile, place the greens and onions in bowls. Top with the steamed asparagus and walnuts. Drizzle with the dressing and serve immediately. Yum!

Serves 4-6
GF/Green/HR
30 Minutes or Under!

♥ Superstars: turmeric (mustard), extra-virgin olive oil, apple cider vinegar, asparagus, greens, onions, walnuts

Broccoli Orange Salad

This pretty, flavorful salad is simple enough for every day yet elegant enough for guests.

- 4 cups broccoli, cut into bite-sized pieces
- ¼ cup raisins
- 3 tablespoons thinly sliced red onion
- 4 teaspoons orange juice
- 2 teaspoons *each:* extra-virgin olive oil and maple syrup (or raw agave nectar)
- 4 medium cloves garlic, minced or pressed
- ½ teaspoon sea salt
- ⅔ cup clementine segments (or seeded orange segments, cut in half)

Optional: Red chili flakes, to taste

1. Steam the broccoli until bright green and crisp-tender, about 4 minutes. Remove from heat and place in a large bowl.

2. Add the remaining ingredients and stir well. Serve cold or at room temperature. This will keep, refrigerated in an airtight container, for several days.

Serves 2-4/GF/SF/Green
30 Minutes or Under!

♥ Superstars: broccoli, onions, extra-virgin olive oil, garlic, chili peppers

Mediterranean Pasta Salad

ıs fresh and delicious salad also doubles as a totally satisfying main dish—at ıeast in my world!

- 8 oz. whole grain pasta shells (I use "Ancient Harvest" corn-quinoa pasta)

- 15 oz. can chickpeas, rinsed and drained (1½ cups)
- 15 oz. can quartered artichoke hearts, drained (1½ cups)
- 1 cup *each:* chopped cucumber and grape (or cherry) tomatoes
- ½ cup *each:* diced onion (white or yellow) and chopped kalamata olives
- ¼ cup (packed) fresh basil, cut into ribbons
- 3 tablespoons fresh lemon juice
- 2 tablespoons extra-virgin olive oil
- 4-5 large cloves garlic, minced or pressed
- 1 teaspoon *each:* sea salt and black pepper

- 4 cups baby greens

1. Cook the pasta until al dente, according to the directions on the package. Drain well and set aside.

2. Toss the remaining ingredients (all but the baby greens) in a large bowl. Add the pasta and stir gently to combine. Serve over baby greens and feel the love!

Serves 4-6
GF/SF/Green
30 Minutes or Under!

♥ Superstars: beans, onions, greens, lemon, extra-virgin olive oil, garlic

Almost Raw Quinoa Toss

This garden-fresh dish may require some forethought, but it only takes about 10 minutes of actual work. However, if you prefer, the quinoa can instead be cooked if instant gratification is what you're currently in need of!

- 1 cup dry quinoa
- 15 oz. can chickpeas, rinsed and drained
- 3 tablespoons fresh lemon juice
- 2 tablespoons extra-virgin olive oil
- ½ cup *each:* arugula and kale, both sliced into very fine ribbons
- ¼ cup fresh basil, cut into thin ribbons
- ½ teaspoon sea salt

1. Cover the quinoa with 3 cups of water and let soak overnight (or for 8-12 hours). Pour off the water, rinse, then drain well. Set aside.

2. In a large bowl, stir the remaining ingredients together with the quinoa. Serve cold or at room temperature. This will keep for about 3 days, refrigerated in an airtight container.

Serves about 4
GF/SF/Green/HR

♥ Superstars: quinoa, beans, lemon, extra-virgin olive oil, greens, kale

Zingy Cranberry Ginger Salad

This dish could not be simpler and is a fantastic way to use raw cranberries. Plus, it's incredibly health-boosting, vitalizing, cleansing, and energizing. Basically, radiant love in a bowl is what's going on here.

- 2 c. fresh cranberries, cut in half or chopped coarsely in a food processor
- 20 oz. can crushed pineapple, in its own juice
- 2 tablespoons finely minced ginger
- *Optional:* ½ cup raw walnuts

1. Toss the cranberries together with the pineapple, pineapple juice, and ginger and refrigerate in an airtight container overnight. This will help to sweeten the cranberries—very important!

2. To serve, stir and top with some of the raw walnuts (if using). This will keep for about a week, refrigerated in an airtight container.

Serves 6/GF/SF/Green/HR/F

♥ Superstars: cranberries, ginger, pineapple, walnuts

🍋 Umeboshi Sesame Kale

This incredibly vitalizing dish takes only 5 minutes to prepare and will boost your immune system, give your skin a glow, nourish your digestive tract, and recharge your batteries. This, in case you were curious, is what some might call a "win-win."

- 2 cups (packed) kale, de-stemmed and cut into thin ribbons
- 2 teaspoons fresh lime juice
- 1 scant teaspoon umeboshi (ume plum) vinegar
- 1 teaspoon *each:* toasted sesame oil and toasted sesame seeds

1. Place the kale in a medium bowl and add the lime juice and vinegar. With your hands, massage the juice and vinegar into the kale. This will tenderize it and turn it a darker shade of green.

2. Stir in the sesame oil and seeds. Serve. This will keep, refrigerated in an airtight container, for several days.

Serves 1-2
GF/SF/Green/HR
30 Minutes or Under!

♥ Superstars: kale, lime, umeboshi, sesame

Broccoli Fig Salad

This addictive salad is bursting with calcium (from the figs and broccoli), fiber, omega-3s, and deliciousness. Now it's up to you to decide—is that something you really want more of in your life?

- 1 cup dried figs (about 8 figs), stems removed and quartered
- ¾ cup thinly sliced onion, white or yellow
- ½ cup raw walnuts
- 2 tablespoons *each:* sesame oil (raw, not toasted) and raw agave nectar
- 1 tablespoon dijon mustard
- ½ teaspoon sea salt

- 3 cups broccoli, cut into bite-sized pieces

1. In a medium bowl, place the figs, onion, walnuts, oil, agave, dijon, and salt. Stir well to combine and set aside.

2. Steam the broccoli for 3-5 minutes over medium-high heat, until the broccoli is bright green and crisp tender. Remove from heat immediately and blanch in ice water. Drain well and toss with the remaining ingredients until well combined. Serve cold or at room temperature. This will keep, refrigerated in an airtight container, for several days.

Serves 4/GF/SF/Green/HR
30 Minutes or Under!

♥ Superstars: figs, onions, walnuts, sesame, broccoli

Simple Pickled Beets

This recipe, although insanely simple, is a perennial staple in my house. I love having tangy sliced beets on hand at all times—they're the perfect addition to salads, sandwiches, and wraps. Plus, you don't have to go through the standard canning rigmarole with this recipe, as these babies are refrigerated.

- 4 small-medium beets
- ¾ cup apple cider vinegar
- 1 tablespoon umeboshi (ume plum) vinegar
- 1½ cups water (approximately)

1. Boil the whole beets (unpeeled) in enough water to cover for about 25-30 minutes. A beet is done when a sharp knife inserted in the center proves it tender. Once tender, remove from heat and drain.

2. Rinse the beets under cold water and peel them. This is accomplished either with your fingers (if the beets are in an agreeable mood) or with a vegetable peeler. Remove the ends as well, using a sharp knife.

3. Slice the beets thinly and place in a container—a quart-sized glass mason jar is perfect for this. Add both vinegars to the jar, then fill it the rest of the way up with water (in a quart jar, you will need 1½ cups of water). Place in the fridge and let marinate for a few hours before serving.

4. To serve, simply remove some sliced beets from the jar and do with them what you will, leaving the remaining beets refrigerated in the liquid. These will keep for at least 2 weeks, refrigerated this way.

Makes 2¼ cups beets
GF/SF/Green

♥ Superstars: beets, apple cider vinegar, umeboshi

Basic Grilled Asparagus

Basically, I never want to eat anything else.

- 2 cups asparagus, trimmed and cut into 2-inch pieces
- 2 teaspoons extra-virgin olive oil
- ¼ teaspoon seasoned salt

1. Preheat your oven to 400° F.

2. Place the asparagus on a baking sheet. Drizzle with the oil and sprinkle with the salt. Shake the pan to distribute the oil and salt evenly onto the asparagus.

3. Bake for 10 minutes. Remove from the oven and shake the pan (or turn the asparagus over). Bake for another 5-10 minutes, or until the asparagus is tender and there are sexy brown flecks in it. Enjoy your veggie paradise!

Serves 1-2
GF/SF/Green
30 Minutes or Under!

♥ Superstars: asparagus, extra-virgin olive oi

Garlic Lover's Broccoli

Roasted garlic + broccoli = YES.

- 6 large cloves garlic, peeled and thinly sliced
- 4 cups broccoli, cut into bite-sized pieces
- 4 teaspoons extra-virgin olive oil
- ¼ teaspoon sea salt

1. Preheat your oven to 400° F.

2. In a large bowl, combine all of the ingredients and stir well. Place on a baking sheet in a single layer, so that the items don't overlap.

3. Bake for 10 minutes. Remove from the oven and stir. Once again, even out the items so that they don't overlap. Bake for another 10-15 minutes, or until the broccoli is very tender, with dark brown flecks, and the garlic is golden-browned. Remove and serve immediately.

Serves 2-4
GF/SF/Green
30 Minutes or Under!

♥ Superstars: garlic, broccoli, extra-virgin olive oil

Citrus Beets with Maple Orange Walnuts

Mmm, come to mama. Seriously, get over here *immediately*. And by the way, I dare you not to eat any of the Maple Orange Walnuts before they find their way onto a beet—I'm quite convinced it can't be done.

- 5-6 medium beets, lightly washed

Mmmarinade:
- ¼ cup fresh orange juice
- 1 tablespoon *each:* fresh lime juice, maple syrup, and olive oil
- 1 teaspoon minced lime zest
- ½ teaspoon minced fresh rosemary
- ¼ teaspoon sea salt

Maple Orange Walnuts:
- 1 cup raw walnuts pieces
- 3 tablespoons maple syrup
- 1½ teaspoons minced orange zest
- ⅛ teaspoon sea salt

Optional: 2 cups baby arugula

1. Place the beets in a large pot and cover them with water. Bring to a boil over high heat. Reduce heat to low and simmer until a sharp knife inserted into the beets proves them tender. Drain and rinse with cold water. Next, peel the beets using a vegetable peeler (or your fingers if the beets are cooperating—they have their moods). With a sharp knife, remove the tough ends of each beet. Finally, thinly slice the beets and set them aside in a bowl.

2. Stir the "Mmmarinade" ingredients together and pour over the cooked, sliced beets. Toss gently and let marinate for an hour or longer.

3. Preheat the oven to 350° F. In a bowl, stir together the walnuts, 3 tablespoons of maple syrup, orange zest, and ⅛ teaspoon of salt. Spread the walnut mixture out evenly on a silicone sheet (ideally) or a nonstick pan. Bake, stirring every 5 minutes, for 15 minutes. Once golden-browned and fully gooey, remove from the oven and stir again. When slightly cooled, remove from the pan and spread out on waxed paper—don't wait too long if you're not using a silicone sheet, or the nuts will stick to your pan. Set aside.

4. *To serve:* Place arugula on plates and top with the beets and some of their marinade. Sprinkle with the walnuts just before serving so they remain crunchy. *Note:* You may have extra walnuts left over. You're welcome.

Serves 4-6
GF/SF/Blue

♥ Superstars: beets, walnuts, citrus zest, lime, greens (arugula)

R.O.C.K. The Top

It's all about the texture with this simple topping. Sprinkle it over any and all Mexican dishes, Thai curries, Indian curries, and Asian noodle bowls. Not only highly nutritious, it's loaded with flavor and fun! (By the way, r.o.c.k. stands for "red onion cilantro kale.")

- 1 cup *each:* finely minced red onion and finely chopped cilantro
- ¼ cup very finely chopped lacinato kale

In a medium bowl, gently stir all of the ingredients together until thoroughly combined. This will keep, refrigerated in an airtight container, for up to 3 days.

Makes 2¼ cups of topping
GF/SF/Green/R
30 Minutes or Under!

♥ Superstars: onions, cilantro, kale

Divine Entrées

This chapter contains proof positive that healthy, plant-based main dishes can be sublimely satisfying. Whether you're in the mood for a comforting one-bowl dish or an elegant crowd-pleaser, these vitalizing, fiber-rich dishes are sure to deliver!

Black-eyed Pea and Potato Tacos

What is it about black-eyed peas and potatoes? In my world, the compatibility of this savory combination rivals peanut butter and jelly. Add some cilantro, onion, and lime and there you have it—perfection on a plate! Incidentally, this recipe works great either as crunchy or soft tacos.

- 1 cup dry black-eyed peas
- 2½ cups water
- 4-inch piece of kombu, optional
- ½ teaspoon sea salt
- 4 medium-large cloves garlic, pressed or minced

- 4 small potatoes, baked and chopped (2¼ cups chopped potatoes, skins on)
- ½ cup minced onion (white or yellow)
- 2 tablespoons fresh lime juice
- 3 tablespoons chopped kalamata olives
- 1 tablespoon extra-virgin olive oil
- ½ teaspoon sea salt
- ¼ teaspoon *each:* ground turmeric and ground cayenne

- 6 crunchy organic taco shells *or* soft corn tortillas
- ½ cup *each:* minced fresh cilantro and minced red onion
- One lime, cut into wedges

1. In a pressure cooker (or pot with a tight fitting lid), place the black-eyed peas, water, and kombu. Bring to a boil, then simmer until the peas are tender. In a pressure cooker, this will take about 40 minutes. In a regular pot, it will take about an hour. Remove from heat and discard the kombu. Stir in the salt and garlic and set aside.

2. Bake the potatoes if you haven't already. In a 400° F oven, this will take about 30 minutes. Once the potatoes are tender, chop into small pieces and combine with the onion (white or yellow), lime juice, olives, oil, salt, turmeric, and cayenne. Stir well and set aside.

3. *For crunchy tacos:* Place a little of the black-eyed peas in each crunchy taco shell. Add some of the potato mixture and top with cilantro and minced red onion. Squeeze a lime wedge over the top and serve immediately. Happy crunching!

4. *For soft tacos:* Warm the soft corn tortillas in a skillet and fill with black-eyed peas, some of the potato mixture, cilantro, and red onion. Squeeze a lime wedge over the top and serve. Happy munching!

Serves 3-6 (makes 6 tacos)
GF/SF/Green

♥ Superstars: beans, sea vegetables (kombu), garlic, onions, lime, extra-virgin olive oil, turmeric, chili peppers (cayenne), cilantro

Fresh and Fast Thai Tofu Bowl

This colorful dish combines cooked and raw items for a fresh, fast, delicious entrée. It may look like a lot of ingredients, but this really does come together very easily, and the entire dish can be prepared while the rice is cooking.

Rice:
- 2 cups water
- 1 cup forbidden rice (or long grain brown rice)
- 2 teaspoons tamari

Simple Sesame Tofu:
- 16 oz. tofu, firm or extra firm (use sprouted tofu if possible)
- ¼ cup tamari
- 2 teaspoons garlic granules
- 2 tablespoons sesame seeds
- 2 teaspoons coconut oil

Fresh Veggies:
- 2 medium carrots, grated (1 cup grated carrots)
- 1 cup finely chopped or shredded cabbage, green or purple
- 4 scallions, trimmed and chopped

Final Flavors:
- ½ cup Thai sweet red chili sauce
- ¼ cup dry-roasted peanuts
- ¼ cup (packed) fresh basil, cut into thin ribbons

1. Place the water, rice, and the 2 teaspoons tamari in a pressure cooker, rice cooker, or pot with a tight fitting lid. Cover and bring to a boil over high heat. Reduce heat to low and simmer until the rice is tender (about 20 minutes in a pressure cooker or 45 minutes otherwise).

2. While the rice is cooking, get the tofu ready for action. Slice into 8 slabs and place on paper towels in a single layer. Cover with more paper towels and place a cutting board or cookie sheet over the top. Weight it down with something heavy such as a gallon of water or a case of strawberry kombucha.

3. While the tofu is pressing, prepare the rest of your ingredients and set them aside. To crush the peanuts (and trust me, you want them crushed), place them in a sealed plastic bag. Roll over the bag with a rolling pin or smash the bag with another heavy object. My daughter finds a large spoon quite fun and effective for this task. Set aside.

4. *To finish the tofu:* Remove the tofu from the pressing situation it's in and cut into ½-inch cubes or little triangles—and yes, technically speaking, triangles are cuter. Next, place in a single layer on a plate and sprinkle with the ¼ cup tamari. Turn the pieces so that they're evenly coated with the tamari. Sprinkle evenly with the garlic granules and sesame seeds. Heat a large skillet or wok over medium-high heat and add the coconut oil. When melted, add the tofu and stir-fry for about 5 minutes, or until the tofu is golden-browned on all sides.

5. *To bowl up your entrée:* Place some rice in each bowl and top with carrots, cabbage, and scallions. Place some tofu on top of that and drizzle with some Sweet Red Chili Sauce. Sprinkle with peanuts and basil and serve immediately.

Serves 4/GF/Green

♥ Superstars: forbidden rice, coconut, carrots, cabbage, sesame, onions (scallions)

Springtime Stir-fry

This fresh, quick entrée comes together in just minutes if you have a cooked, cold baked potato on hand. I love the fact that everything you need is right here in one dish—complex carbohydrates, fiber-rich veggies, and vitalizing superfoods. Yeah, baby!

- One medium cold baked potato, chopped (1¼ cups chopped potato)
- 2 teaspoons extra-virgin olive oil

- 1 cup asparagus, trimmed and chopped into 1-inch pieces
- 2 scallions, trimmed and chopped into 1-inch pieces (⅓ cup)

- 1 teaspoon (packed) minced lemon zest (zest of about one lemon)
- 2 medium cloves garlic, pressed or minced
- 1 tablespoon chopped kalamata olives
- ¼ teaspoon sea salt
- Freshly ground black pepper, to taste

1. Set a wok or skillet to medium-high heat and add the potato and oil. Stir-fry for 5 minutes, or until the potato chunks are lightly browned.

2. Add the asparagus and stir-fry for 3 minutes, or until it's *almost* crisp-tender and bright green.

3. Add the scallions and stir-fry for an additional minute, or until the scallions and asparagus are crisp-tender and bright green. Remove from heat and stir in the remaining ingredients. Serve immediately.

Serves 1-2/GF/SF/Green
30 Minutes or Under! (needs a cold, cooked potato)

♥ Superstars: extra-virgin olive oil, asparagus, onions (scallions), citrus zest, garlic

🍋 Lemon Asparagus Quinoa Toss

Hello, new BFF!

- 2 cups asparagus, trimmed and cut into 1-inch pieces
- 1 teaspoon extra-virgin olive oil

- ½ cup dry quinoa
- 1 cup water
- 1 tablespoon *each:* fresh lemon juice and additional extra-virgin olive oil
- 1 teaspoon (packed) minced lemon zest (zest of about one large lemon)
- 2 medium-large cloves garlic, minced or pressed
- ¼ teaspoon *each:* sea salt and black pepper

1. Preheat the oven to 400° F. Place the asparagus on a baking sheet and drizzle with the 1 teaspoon of oil. Shake the pan to coat the asparagus with the oil. Bake for 10 minutes. Remove from the oven and shake the pan again (to turn the asparagus). Bake for another 10 minutes, or until the asparagus is tender and roasted.

2. Meanwhile, place the quinoa and water in a covered pot and bring to a boil over high heat. Reduce heat to low and simmer until the water has been absorbed and the quinoa is tender, about 15 minutes.

3. While the asparagus and quinoa are doing their thang, you can get your groove on with the rest of this dish. In a medium bowl, place the remaining ingredients and stir well.

4. Add the asparagus and quinoa to the bowl and stir everything together well. Serve warm, at room temperature, or cold.

Serves 2/GF/SF/Green/30 Minutes or Under!

♥ Superstars: asparagus, extra-virgin olive oil, quinoa, lemon, citrus zest, garlic

Wild Rice and White Bean Fritters

These are perhaps one of the best ways to fritter away your time.

- ½ cup dry white beans, soaked for 8-12 hours in plenty of water to cover
- ¼ cup dry wild rice
- 1¾ cups water
- 4-inch piece kombu, optional but awesome

- 2 cups whole grain bread crumbs (3 slices "Food For Life" Ezekiel sprouted grain bread, whirred in a food processor)
- ¼ cup *each:* cornmeal, minced onion, chopped cilantro, and lemon juice
- 3 large cloves garlic, minced or pressed
- 2 tablespoons dry polenta meal
- 1 tablespoon minced lemon zest
- 2 teaspoons salt-free Cajun seasoning
- 1½ teaspoons sea salt
- 1 teaspoon *each:* ground black pepper and smoked paprika

For pan-frying: extra-virgin olive oil or non-virgin coconut oil

1. Drain the water off of the beans. Place in a pressure cooker (or pot with a tight fitting lid) along with the rice, water, and kombu. Bring to a boil over high heat. Reduce heat to low and simmer, covered, until the beans and rice are tender. This will take about 25 minutes in a pressure cooker or 1 hour in a regular pot. Remove from heat and drain off any excess water. Remove the kombu.

2. In a large bowl, mix the rice and beans with the remaining ingredients. Stir well until thoroughly combined.

3. Set a large skillet to medium heat and add a little oil. Form the mixture into small patties and pan-fry until golden-browned on each side. Serve hot or warm.

Serves 4/SF/Green/F

♥ Superstars: beans, sea vegetables (kombu), onions, cilantro, lemons, garlic, citrus zest

 # Tropical Curry Slurry

This delicious, nutrient-dense entrée is a cross between a soup and a curry. It's great as a one dish meal—the epitome of yummy, satisfying comfort food.

- 14 oz. can lowfat coconut milk
- 1 teaspoon red curry paste (I use "Thai Kitchen" brand)
- Two 15 oz. cans black beans, rinsed and drained
- 1 cup cooked brown rice
- 1 cup chopped ripe banana (one large banana)
- 3 tablespoons fresh lime juice
- 2 tablespoons grated ginger
- 1 tablespoon raw agave nectar
- 3 large cloves garlic, minced or pressed
- 1 teaspoon sea salt

Garnishes:
- 4 tablespoons chopped cilantro
- 4 teaspoons dry-roasted peanuts, crushed

1. In a small bowl, combine the curry paste with a little of the coconut milk. Whisk or stir until emulsified and no lumps remain.

2. Place in a medium pot along with the beans, remaining coconut milk, and rice. Set to medium heat and cook for 5 minutes, stirring often.

3. Add the remaining ingredients (all but the garnishes) and reduce heat to low. Stir and cook for 2-3 minutes, until the bananas are soft and the mixture is warm.

4. Serve in bowls, topped with the cilantro and peanuts. Leftovers will store for about a week, refrigerated in an airtight container. Please note that any leftovers will thicken up considerably, so add a little coconut milk or water if needed.

Serves 4/GF/SF/Green/F/30 Minutes or Under! (needs cooked rice)

♥ Superstars: coconut, chili peppers (curry paste), beans, lime, ginger, garlic, cilantro

Happiness Bowl

Why will this dish make you happy? Well, it's everything you could possibly need, right there in a cozy, yummy bowl. Plus, I just adore the idea of combining cooked and raw foods—you get the best of both worlds that way. Finally, comfort food that loves you back!

- 1 recipe "Everyday Chicky Gravy" (p. 64)
- 4 cups cooked brown rice, warm or hot

- 14 oz. firm (or extra-firm) tofu (use sprouted tofu if available)
- 2½ tablespoons tamari
- 2 teaspoons garlic granules
Optional: 4 teaspoons nutritional yeast

- 4 teaspoons non-virgin coconut oil (or olive oil)

- 4 cups sliced shiitake mushroom caps
- 2 cups *each:* baby spinach (or chopped chard), grated carrots, and shredded cabbage

1. Prepare the gravy and cook the rice if you haven't yet done so. Set them aside, keeping warm if possible.

2. Slice the tofu into ½-inch thick slabs and press with paper towels to remove excess moisture. Cut into ½-inch cubes or little triangles, depending on your mood (plain or fancy). Sprinkle evenly with the tamari and garlic granules (and nutritional yeast, if using) and toss gently to coat.

3. In a large skillet or wok, heat the coconut oil over medium-high heat. Add the tofu and stir-fry for 3-5 minutes, or until golden-browned. Remove to a plate.

4. Add the shiitake mushrooms to the skillet and stir-fry until browned and tender. If necessary, add another teaspoon of oil or a little water to prevent sticking. Remove from heat.

5. *To serve:* Place some rice in the bottom of each bowl. Top with spinach (or chard), carrots, cabbage, and warm shiitake mushrooms. Sprinkle with tofu cubes and top with gravy. Serve immediately.

Serves 4-6/GF/Green

♥ Superstars: nutritional yeast, coconut, shiitake mushrooms, greens, carrots, cabbage

> ### Hint:
> For an extra-special treat, serve topped with caramelized shallots (or onions) and a sprinkle or sprig of fresh rosemary.

Asian Quinoa Wraps

These wraps are mostly raw, totally easy to make, and completely delicious! Although the quinoa requires an overnight soak, these wraps will come together in a flash. As a variation, you can also serve the quinoa mixture over a bed of greens as a salad, topped with the peanuts.

- 1 cup quinoa, soaked in plenty of water to cover for 8-12 hours

- ½ cup *each:* chopped scallions and grated carrots
- ¼ cup chopped cilantro
- 2 tablespoons raw agave nectar
- 1 tablespoon *each:* tamari, toasted sesame oil, lime juice, and grated ginger
- 2 medium cloves garlic, pressed or minced

- 6 chard or romaine lettuce leaves
- 3 tablespoons dry-roasted peanuts, crushed

1. Rinse and drain the quinoa. In a large bowl, toss it with the scallions, carrots, cilantro, agave, tamari, oil, lime, ginger, and garlic. Stir well to combine.

2. Place a scoop of the quinoa mixture in the center of each chard or romaine leaf. The mixture is a bit saucy, so feel free to drizzle some of the shizzle (sauce) all up in there as well. Top with some of the peanuts, wrap the leaf around the filling, and serve. The quinoa mixture will keep, refrigerated in an airtight container, for several days.

Serves 3/GF/Green/HR
30 Minutes or Under! (needs soaked quinoa)

♥ Superstars: quinoa, onions (scallions), carrots, cilantro, sesame, lime, ginger, garlic, greens

Sweet and Simple Glazed Tempeh

In this one-pan entrée, tempeh is made delicious with the simplest of treatments. This works well as a side, main dish, sandwich or wrap filling, topping for salads, or stir-fry component. The idea for this dish originally came from my "kynd tempeh burgers" I used to make for Grateful Dead shows. I would put this tempeh on a whole grain bun and top it generously with tahini, sliced red onions, and lettuce—and, yes, I always sold out!

- 8 oz. tempeh, cut into cubes
- ¼ cup water
- 2 tablespoons *each:* tamari and raw agave nectar
- 2 teaspoons toasted (dark) sesame oil
- 2 large cloves garlic, minced or pressed

1. Heat a wok or skillet over medium-high heat. Add the tempeh and water. Cover and steam until there is no more water (in the pan, that is—there should still be water elsewhere in the world when you're done).

2. Uncover and add the tamari, agave, and oil. Stir-fry until the tempeh is golden-browned and looks caramelized in parts. Remove from heat. Add the garlic and stir gently to combine. Do with it what you will.

Serves 2-3
GF/Green/F
30 Minutes or Under!

♥ Superstars: tempeh, sesame, garlic

Green Tea and Pineapple Rice with Coconut Tofu

I know this dish may look complicated, but it comes together in only 30 minutes if you have a pressure cooker. It's very pretty and contains a plethora of nutrient-dense superfoods to keep your body buzzing with vitality!

Green Tea and Pineapple Rice:
- 4 green tea teabags
- 2 cups *each:* boiling water, long grain brown rice, and pineapple juice
- 1 cup chopped pineapple (or drained pineapple tidbits)
- 3 tablespoons fresh lime juice
- 2 tablespoons raw agave nectar
- 1½ teaspoons sea salt

Coconut Tofu:
- 14 oz. tofu, firm or extra-firm (use sprouted tofu if available)
- 2 tablespoons tamari
- ½ cup finely shredded coconut
- ¼ cup sesame seeds, preferably black
- ½ teaspoon sea salt
- 2 tablespoons coconut oil

Golden Garlic Heaven:
- 2 teaspoons coconut oil
- ½ cup thinly sliced garlic (about 12 large cloves garlic)

Gingered Cabbage:
- 2 teaspoons coconut oil
- 4 cups thinly shredded (not grated) green cabbage
- 4 scallions (green onions), trimmed and chopped
- ¼ cup minced fresh ginger
- ¾ teaspoon ground turmeric
- ½ teaspoon sea salt

1. *To make the rice:* Place the teabags in a pressure cooker or large pot that has a tight fitting lid. Pour the boiling water into the pot and let steep for 15 minutes. Squeeze the teabags into the pot and then discard them. Add the rice and pineapple juice to the tea in the pot, cover tightly, and bring to a boil over high heat. Reduce heat to low and simmer until the rice is tender (about 20 minutes in a pressure cooker or 45 minutes in a regular pot). Stir in the remaining "Green Tea and Pineapple Rice" items and set aside.

2. *While the rice is cooking:* Slice the tofu into 8 cutlets. Place 2-3 layers of paper towels on a countertop and lay the cutlets over them in a single layer. Cover with more layered paper towels and place a cutting board or cookie sheet on top. Place weights on top of that and let the tofu press for at least 15 minutes. Next, cut the tofu into cubes, place on a plate, and sprinkle with the tamari. Set aside.

3. *Golden Garlic Heaven:* In a large skillet or wok, heat the 2 teaspoons of coconut oil over medium heat. Add the garlic and stir-fry for several minutes, stirring often, until the garlic is a lovely light golden brown color. Remove immediately to a plate as the garlic will turn bitter if cooked too long. Set aside.

4. *To finish the tofu:* Place the shredded coconut, sesame seeds, and the ½ teaspoon sea salt in a large plastic bag and seal tightly. Shake well to combine. Add the tofu and shake gently to coat with the coconut "breading." Heat the previously used skillet or wok over medium heat and add the 2 tablespoons of coconut oil. Once it's melted, add the tofu and cook, stirring gently every few minutes, until the tofu is golden-browned on all sides. This should take about 5-7 minutes. Remove to a plate and set aside.

5. *Gingered Cabbage:* Wipe the inside of the skillet or wok with a paper towel to remove any debris. Heat over medium heat and add the 2 teaspoons of coconut oil. When melted, add the cabbage, scallions, ginger, turmeric, and ½ teaspoon of salt. Stir-fry for about 2 minutes and remove from heat.

6. *To serve:* Place a scoop of rice in each bowl and top with gingered cabbage. Place some of the tofu on top and sprinkle with the golden garlic. Serve.

Serves 6/GF/Blue/30 Minutes or Under! (if using a pressure cooker)

♥ Superstars: green tea, pineapple, lime, coconut, sesame, garlic, cabbage, onions (scallions), ginger, turmeric

Hungarian Chickpeas

Welcome to my new obsession.

- 15 oz. can chickpeas (garbanzo beans), rinsed and drained
- 2 tablespoons pitted and quartered kalamata olives (or other Greek olives)
- 2 tablespoons *each:* raisins, chopped cilantro, and minced yellow or white onion
- 1 tablespoon *each:* extra-virgin olive oil and raw agave nectar
- 2 teaspoons *each:* dijon mustard, fresh lime juice, and smoked paprika
- 1 teaspoon dried oregano
- 2 large cloves garlic, minced or pressed
- ½ teaspoon sea salt

Combine all of the ingredients and stir very well. Serve cold or at room temperature. This will keep, refrigerated in an airtight container, for up to a week.

Serves 2/GF/SF/Green
30 Minutes or Under!

♥ Superstars: beans, cilantro, onions, extra-virgin olive oil, lime, garlic

10 Minute Kalesadillas

Here's the perfect way to pack all kinds of superfoods into a quick, yummy lunch. Obviously, if you're making the optional toppings from scratch, the time limit will exceed 10 minutes on this dish. However, if you're a Mexican food junkie like me, it's likely you'll already have them leftover in your fridge, just waiting for a chance like this.

- 2 sprouted corn tortillas (approximately 6-inches in size)
- 2 medium cloves garlic, pressed or minced
- ⅓ cup organic vegetarian refried beans
- ¼ cup *each:* thinly sliced kale and shredded vegan cheese (I use "Daiya")
- ½ teaspoon coconut oil

Optional toppings:
- ¼ cup "Pretty Pico" (p. 66) or salsa
- ¼ cup "R.O.C.K. The Top" (p. 130)
- 3 tablespoons "Green Velvet Guacamole" (p. 77) or guacamole of your choice

1. Spread the garlic evenly over one of the tortillas. Prepare all of the other items you'll be using.

2. Preheat a medium skillet over medium heat, add the coconut oil, and let it melt. Place the beans on the tortilla (on top of the garlic), then top evenly with the kale and cheese. Cover with the remaining tortilla.

3. Place on the skillet and cover with a lid. Cook for 3 minutes, then gently flip over. Cook for another 3 minutes, or until both sides are lightly browned.

4. Serve immediately, topped with any or all of the optional toppings.

**Serves 1/GF/SF (without "Green Velvet Guacamole")/Green
30 Minutes or Under!**

♥ Superstars (not including optional toppings): sprouted grains (tortillas), garlic, beans, kale, coconut

Feel Fabulous Noodles

Eat these delicious, immune-boosting noodles whenever you want to stave off a cold, build up your health, or just enjoy some insanely delicious comfort food.

Black Sesame Tofu:
- 14 oz. firm or extra-firm tofu (preferably sprouted tofu)
- 2 tablespoons tamari
- ¼ cup black sesame seeds (or regular sesame seeds)
- 1 tablespoon non-virgin coconut oil

- 8 oz. whole grain linguine or spaghetti (I use "Ancient Harvest" corn-quinoa noodles)

Superfood Sauce:
- 5 tablespoons fresh lemon juice
- 4 tablespoons toasted (dark) sesame oil
- 3 tablespoons *each:* grated fresh ginger and mellow white miso
- 2 tablespoons tamari
- 4 large cloves garlic, pressed or finely minced

Vivacious Veggies:
- 1 cup shelled edamame, thawed if frozen
- 1 cup chopped scallions (trimmed and cut into 1-inch pieces)
- 1 medium carrot (½ cup), finely chopped or julienne cut

Garnish: ½ cup chopped fresh cilantro

1. Drain the tofu and slice it into 8 slabs. Lay the slabs out flat on paper towels and cover with more paper towels (or tea towels). Cover with a baking sheet or large cutting board and place weights over the top. This step of pressing the tofu will give it a firmer texture and help it to absorb the marinade better. Let the tofu press for at least 10 minutes (or up to several hours).

2. Meanwhile, cook the noodles according to the directions on their package (tending toward the al dente side—we don't want mushy noodles!) and drain. Set aside.

3. While the noodles are cooking, place the sauce ingredients in a very large bowl. Combine well using a whisk. Be sure to remove all of the lumps from the miso. Set aside.

4. Cut each tofu slab in half, then into small triangles so that you end up with 32 tofu triangles. Sprinkle with the 2 tablespoons of tamari and turn each piece until all of the tamari is absorbed into the tofu. Scatter the sesame seeds on top.

5. In a large skillet or wok, heat the coconut oil over medium-high heat. Add the tofu (and all of the seeds, if any have tried to escape). Stir-fry, gently turning occasionally, for about 5 minutes, or until lightly browned on all sides. Remove to a plate.

6. *Final matter of bizness:* Add the noodles and vegetables to the sauce and stir well to combine. Serve topped with tofu triangles and cilantro. Say hello to Mr. Delicious.

Serves 4
GF/Blue/HR

♥ Superstars: sesame, coconut, lemon, sesame, ginger, miso, garlic, edamame, onions (scallions), carrots, cilantro

Smoky One Pot Beans and Rice

This dish is all at once easy, healthy, scrumptious, addictive, and satisfying. And that's how much I love you.

- 1 cup long grain brown rice
- 2 cups water
- ¼ cup "Chicky Baby Seasoning" (p. 67)

- 1 cup lightly packed kale, de-stemmed and cut into thin ribbons
- 15 oz. can black or red beans, rinsed and drained
- 2 tablespoons extra-virgin olive oil
- 4 large cloves garlic, pressed or minced
- 1 teaspoon liquid smoke
- ½ teaspoon sea salt

1. In a pressure cooker or pot with a tight fitting lid, place the rice, water, and "Chicky Baby Seasoning." Bring to a boil over high heat, then simmer over low heat until the rice is tender and the water is fully absorbed. In a pressure cooker, this will take about 20 minutes. In a regular pot, it will take about 45 minutes.

2. Once the rice is done, stir in the kale immediately so that it wilts from the heat. Add all of the remaining ingredients, stir well, and feel loved—because you are! Leftovers will store, refrigerated in an airtight container, for about a week.

Serves 4
GF/SF/Green/F
30 Minutes or Under! (if using a pressure cooker)

♥ Superstars: nutritional yeast, kale, beans, extra-virgin olive oil, garlic

Our Daily Pizza

Yes, it's true. I make these almost every day. They really satisfy that pizza craving, all while providing loads of uber-healthy nutrients—plus, they're even low in calories. Win!

- One sprouted grain English muffin (I use "Food For Life" Ezekiel muffins)
- Organic, vegan pizza (or pasta) sauce, to taste
- ¼ cup shredded vegan cheese (I use "Daiya" brand)
- 2 medium-large garlic cloves, peeled and thinly sliced
- One shiitake mushroom cap, thinly sliced
- 2 tablespoons kale, cut into thin ribbons

1. Preheat your oven to 400° F.

2. Split the English muffin in half and top each open-facing side with pizza sauce. Sprinkle the vegan cheese evenly on top. Add the toppings and bake for 15-20 minutes, or until lightly browned. Serve immediately.

Serves 1/SF/Green
30 Minutes or Under!

♥ Superstars: sprouted grains, garlic, shiitake mushrooms, kale

 # Immune Boon Noodles

Did you just spend 4 hours on a plane next to a coughing, sneezing, sweaty man? If so, you have my deepest sympathies. But, hey! If you whip up a batch of this, it'll be like it never happened. Heartier than miso soup, these noodles are delicious and power-packed to keep you healthy, even in the worst of circumstances!

- 14 oz. firm or extra-firm tofu (preferably sprouted)
- 2 tablespoons tamari
- 2 teaspoons toasted (dark) sesame oil

- 8 oz. whole grain noodles (I use "Ancient Harvest" corn-quinoa spaghetti)

Miso in Love With Ginger Sauce:
- 2 tablespoons tamari
- 1 tablespoon *each:* grated ginger, miso (red or dark), toasted sesame oil, and fresh lime juice
- 4 large cloves garlic, minced or pressed
- ¼ teaspoon red chili flakes (or more to taste)

Stir-fry:
- 1 cup *each:* sliced shiitake mushroom caps and shelled edamame
- 5 scallions, trimmed and cut into 1-inch pieces

Last Additions:
- ½ cup chopped fresh cilantro
- ¼ cup toasted sesame seeds (dry toasted until lightly browned)

1. Cut the tofu into 8 slabs and lay out flat on a clean surface in a single layer. Cover with paper towels (or tea towels) and place a cutting board or cookie sheet over the top. Place weights on top to press the tofu. Let rest for as long as possible, but at least 10 minutes.

2. Meanwhile, prepare the noodles according to the instructions on their package. Once they're al dente, drain and set aside.

3. While the noodles are cooking, stir the ingredients for the sauce together in a small bowl. Be sure to remove any lumps from the miso. Set aside.

4. It's tofu brownin' time! Disassemble the tofu pressing station and cut the tofu into 1-inch cubes. In a large skillet or wok, heat the 2 teaspoons of sesame oil and add the tamari. Add the tofu and toss gently to coat. Stir-fry for about 5 minutes, turning often, until the tofu is golden-browned on all sides. Remove to a plate.

5. In the same skillet or wok, stir-fry the shiitake mushrooms (adding just a little water if needed) for 3-5 minutes, or until soft. Add the edamame and scallions and cook for 1-2 more minutes.

6. Place the noodles in a large bowl and gently toss with the sauce. Add the stir-fried vegetables, cilantro, and sesame seeds. Stir gently until thoroughly combined. Serve topped with the tofu. This is good hot, warm, or cold.

Serves 6
GF/Green
30 Minutes or Under!

♥ Superstars: sesame, ginger, miso, lime, garlic, chili peppers, shiitake mushrooms, edamame, onions (scallions), cilantro

Pineapple Tempeh with Red Rice

This delicately flavored, beautiful dish is actually quite easy to prepare and comes together while the rice is cooking. If you can't find red rice, you may substitute any other whole grain rice of your choosing.

Red Rice:
- 1 cup dry red jasmine rice
- 2½ cups water
- 1 tablespoon tamari

Roasted Deliciousness:
- 3 cups pineapple chunks, fresh or frozen
- 8 large garlic cloves, peeled and quartered
- 1 teaspoon coconut oil, melted and divided

Tempehtation:
- 8 oz. tempeh, cut into ½-inch cubes
- 1½ - 2 tablespoons tamari
- 1 tablespoon coconut oil
- 1 teaspoon garlic granules

Stir-fry:
- 2 cups lightly packed kale (cut into thin ribbons)
- 5 scallions, trimmed and cut into 1-inch pieces
- 1 teaspoon tamari

Final garnishes:
- ¼ cup finely shredded coconut, toasted in a dry skillet until lightly browned
- One lime, cut into wedges

1. Place the rice, water, and 1 tablespoon of tamari in a rice cooker or pot with a tight fitting lid. Bring to a boil over high heat, then reduce heat to low and simmer for 30 minutes, or until all of the liquids are absorbed and the rice is tender. Set aside (with the lid on) to keep warm.

2. Preheat the oven to 400° F. In a small bowl, toss half of the teaspoon of coconut oil with the pineapple chunks. Place them in a single layer on one end of a baking sheet.

3. In a small bowl, toss the remaining half teaspoon of coconut oil with the quartered garlic cloves. Place in a single layer on the other side of the baking sheet, leaving enough space away from the pineapple to keep any pineapple juice from trespassing onto the garlic.

4. Place the pineapple and garlic in the oven and bake for about 10 minutes, or until the garlic is golden-browned. Remove the garlic and set it aside. Stir the pineapple and place it back in the oven for another 10 minutes, or until it too is golden-browned. Remove and set aside.

5. Set a wok or skillet over medium-high heat. Add the tempeh, tamari, 1 tablespoon of coconut oil, and garlic granules. Stir-fry until the tempeh is browned and crisp, about 5 minutes. Remove to a plate.

6. In the same pan, stir-fry the kale and scallions in the teaspoon of tamari for about a minute, or until the kale is slightly wilted and bright green. Set aside.

7. *To serve:* Place a scoop of rice on a plate and top with some of the kale-scallion mixture. Top evenly with tempeh, pineapple, and garlic. Garnish with coconut and serve with a lime wedge—which I strongly suggest squeezing over the top for maximum flavor. Enjoy!

Serves 4
GF/Green/F

♥ Superstars: red rice, pineapple, garlic, coconut, tempeh, kale, onions

Feel Good Mac 'N Cheese

This creamy macaroni and cheese is totally satisfying, yet devoid of the junk that usually accompanies this comfort food. Plus, the addition of several vitalizing superfoods will leave your soul feeling satisfied and your body feeling nourished!

- 8 oz. whole grain pasta elbows (I use "Ancient Harvest" corn-quinoa pasta)
- ¼ cup *each:* nutritional yeast powder and unsweetened nondairy milk
- 2 tablespoons oil (raw sesame, olive, or melted non-virgin coconut)
- ½ tablespoon mellow white miso
- 1-2 medium cloves garlic, minced or pressed
- 1 teaspoon mustard powder
- ½ teaspoon sea salt

Optional: 2 tablespoons chopped parsley and/or minced chives

1. Boil the pasta until al dente according to the instructions on the package.

2. Meanwhile, whisk all of the remaining ingredients (aside from the parsley) together until very smooth.

3. Once the pasta is done, drain well and toss with the sauce. Serve immediately. If desired, garnish with the parsley and/or chives.

Serves 2-4
GF/Blue
30 Minutes or Under!

♥ Superstars: nutritional yeast, miso, garlic, parsley

Sweet Bliss

These incredibly delicious desserts are the perfect way to get nutrified and satisfied all at once. Made with only natural sweeteners, whole foods, and nutrient-dense ingredients, these sweet treats will leave you feeling guilt-free, nourished, and unreasonably happy!

Key Lime Pie with Coconut Ginger Crust

This pie is raw, vitalizing, nutrient-dense, and exploding with tangy lime flavor. Hopefully this will put the whole "Do you really love me?" thing to rest—because if it's not blatantly obvious after tasting this pie, then I just don't know what.

Coconut Ginger Crust:
- ½ cup *each:* raw almonds, shredded coconut, and raisins
- 1½ teaspoons dried ginger
- ⅛ teaspoon sea salt

Tangy Lime Filling:
- 1½ cups raw cashews, soaked in plenty of water to cover for 8-12 hours
- ½ cup plus 3 tablespoons fresh lime juice
- ½ cup raw agave nectar
- ¼ cup non-virgin coconut oil
- 1 tablespoon lime zest
- 1 teaspoon vanilla extract (optional)
- ¼ teaspoon sea salt

Garnish: additional 1 tablespoon minced lime zest

1. Place all of the Coconut Ginger Crust ingredients in a food processor. Blend until thoroughly combined and crumbly, but don't overdo it—you want to retain a little texture for fun's sake. Pour the mixture into a pie pan and distribute evenly over the bottom. Press the mixture down firmly with the palm of your hand to form an even, solid bottom crust. Cover and place in the freezer.

2. In a blender or food processor, place all of the filling ingredients (except for the garnish). Blend very well, until completely smooth (except for some of the lime zest, which can remain in tact—it's special that way).

3. Remove the crust from the freezer and pour the filling into it. Evenly distribute the filling over the crust and sprinkle the top with the additional 1 tablespoon lime zest. Cover the pan once again. Place in the refrigerator for an hour, or until quite firm. Cut, serve, and feel oh-so loved.

Serves 8/GF/SF/Blue/R/F

♥ Superstars: almonds, coconut, ginger, cashews, lime, citrus zest

Rawkin Superfood Truffles

Roll up your sleeves. This is going to get interesting. And delicious. And vitalizing. You're welcome.

- ¾ cup raw coconut butter
- ½ cup raw cacao powder
- ¼ cup plus 2 tablespoons raw agave nectar
- 1 tablespoon *each:* raw maca powder and chia seeds
- 2 teaspoons vanilla extract
- ½ teaspoon mint extract
- ¼ teaspoon sea salt

Coating: ½ cup raw cacao nibs

1. In a food processor, blend the coconut butter, cacao, agave, maca, chia, vanilla, mint, and salt. When totally smooth, transfer to a container, cover, and place in the freezer. When the mixture is very firm (almost solid, but still workable), remove from the freezer. This should take about 20 minutes.

2. Place the cacao nibs on a plate.

3. Pull out small pieces of the mixture and roll into 1-inch balls with your hands. This is a gooey process—I won't lie to you at this stage of the game. But you can do it. Remember, there's chocolate at the end of this tunnel.

4. Roll each ball in the cacao nibs and place in a container or on a plate. Store, covered, in the refrigerator until ready to serve.

Makes 12 truffles (12 servings)
GF/SF/Blue/R/F/30 Minutes or Under!

♥ Superstars: coconut, cacao, maca, chia

Pineapple Right-Side-Up Cake

Cake a superfood? Oh yeah. It's all about the balance, baby! One of my recipe testing rock stars, Erica Hunter, inspired me with her simple, delicious recipe for pineapple cake. Enjoy!

- 2 cups whole wheat pastry flour
- 1¼ teaspoons baking soda
- ½ teaspoon sea salt
- 3 tablespoons flaxseed meal

- ¼ cup coconut oil
- 20 oz. can pineapple chunks (in their own juice), drained (juice reserved)
- ¾ cup raw agave nectar
- 1 tablespoon apple cider vinegar
- 1 teaspoon vanilla extract

1. Preheat the oven to 350° F. Generously oil an 8 x 8-inch baking pan and set aside. In a medium bowl, place the flour, soda, salt, and flaxseed meal. Whisk together until well mixed. Set aside.

2. In a medium pan, melt the coconut oil. Stir in the pineapple juice (not chunks), agave, vinegar, and vanilla. Stir to combine well. Pour this mixture into the dry mixture. Stir them together gently, *just* until thoroughly combined.

3. Place the pineapple chunks in the bottom of the oiled baking pan. Pour the cake mix over the pineapple chunks into the pan.

4. Bake for 25-35 minutes, or until the cake is very golden-browned and a knife inserted into the center comes out clean. *Important tip:* This cake may look done before it actually *is* done, but if you wait until the knife comes out clean, you'll be golden. Pineapple cake golden, that is.

5. Let the cake cool slightly. To serve, cut into 9 pieces and scoop out each piece, making sure to include the pineapple that's on the bottom. Enjoy!

Serves 9/SF/Blue/F

♥ Superstars: flax, coconut, pineapple, apple cider vinegar

Kick Acai Strawberry Sauce

Holy yum, people. And it's raw! This is great over pancakes, waffles, fruit salads, vegan yogurt, and coconut ice cream. Basically, anything you want to bliss up.

- One 3.5 oz. packet frozen acai (I use "Sambazon" brand)
- 3 cups fresh or frozen strawberries
- ¼ cup raw agave nectar
- 1 teaspoon vanilla extract
- ⅛ teaspoon sea salt

Blend all of the ingredients thoroughly in your blender. That's it! You are now ready to pour this over anything your heart desires. This will keep, refrigerated in an airtight container, for at least a week.
Makes 3 cups (serves 12)/GF/SF/Green/R/F/30 Minutes or Under!

♥ Superstars: acai, strawberries

Maca Chip Cookies

- ½ cup (packed) pitted dried dates (12 dates)
- ¼ cup *each:* raw cashews, raw almonds, and rolled oats
- 2 tablespoons raw maca powder
- 1 tablespoon *each:* vanilla and raw agave nectar
- ¼ teaspoon sea salt
Add last: 2 tablespoons raw cacao nibs

In a food processor, blend all of the ingredients except for the cacao nibs. When the mixture is in fine crumbs and very sticky, remove and stir in the nibs. Form into balls, then shape into cookies. Heaven!
Makes 12 cookies (6 servings)/GF/SF/Blue/R/F/30 Minutes or Under!

♥ Superstars: cashews, almonds, maca, cacao

Mango Paradise Bars

Think of this recipe as a healthy energy treat that can also double as a light, yet thoroughly satisfying dessert. In paradise.

- 1½ cups raw cashews
- ¼ cup fresh lime juice
- 3 cups ripe mango flesh
- ⅔ cup raw coconut butter
- ½ cup *each:* fresh lemon juice and raw agave nectar
- ½ teaspoon sea salt

1. Soak the cashews in water for 8-12 hours (or overnight). Drain and set aside.

2. In a food processor or blender, combine the cashews with the lime juice and blend until as smooth as possible. Add the remaining ingredients and blend until very smooth.

3. Pour/scrape into a large glass baking dish (lasagna sized, about 9 x 14-inches). Spread out evenly and cover. Place into the freezer for several hours until hardened.

4. Cut into 20 squares and serve icy cold, right out of the freezer.

Makes 20 servings
GF/SF/Blue/R/F

♥ Superstars: mango, lime, lemon, coconut

Raw Carob Maca Chocolate

Looking for the ultimate health-supporting chocolate bar? Yeah, I figured you were. That's why I went ahead and whipped up this recipe. Not only is this as easy as toast to make (well, almost), it's **crazy** good for you.

- ¼ cup (packed) pitted dates (about 8 dates)
- ¼ cup raw agave nectar
- 3 tablespoons *each:* carob powder, raw cacao powder, and coconut oil
- 2 tablespoons raw maca powder
- ¼ teaspoon sea salt

1. In a food processor, blend all of the ingredients until completely smooth.

2. Transfer the chocolate onto a plate or waxed paper and form into a ¼-inch thick slab. If this is too tricky, you can first place the mixture into the freezer until it thickens up a bit.

3. Once your mixture is in slab formation, place in the freezer for 20 minutes, or until firm. From there, cut it into 6 pieces and refrigerate in an airtight container.

Serves 6/GF/SF/Blue/R/F
30 Minutes or Under!

♥ Superstars: carob, cacao, coconut, maca

Raw Cacao Superfood Pie

Deliciousness squared. Well, actually rounded, but you get the idea. This health-supporting pie is a great way to satisfy your chocolate tooth while still feeding your body lots of powerful nutrients. Aside from soaking the cashews, this pie will come together in about 20 minutes. Score!

Almond Maca Crust:
- 1 cup raw almonds
- ½ cup (packed) dried dates, pitted (about 8 dates)
- 4 dried figs (⅓ cup), stems removed
- 2 tablespoons raw maca powder
- ¼ teaspoon sea salt

Cacao Filling:
- 1½ cups raw cashews, soaked in plenty of water to cover (for 8-10 hours)
- ¾ cup raw agave nectar
- ½ cup raw coconut butter
- ¼ cup raw cacao powder
- 1 tablespoon vanilla extract
- ½ teaspoon sea salt

Topping:
- ½ cup raw cacao nibs

1. In a food processor, blend the crust ingredients until they begin to ball up. You want the mixture to be sticky, but still crumbly.

2. Pour into an ungreased pie pan and press to form a crust, making sure to bring the sides up as well. Press well, using your hands, paying special attention to the place where the bottom connects to the sides. Cover and put in the freezer.

3. Drain the cashews. In a food processor, blend all of the "Cacao Filling" items until very smooth. Remove the crust from the freezer and pour the filling into it.

4. Top the pie with the cacao nibs and refrigerate for 2 hours before serving.

Serves 8/GF/SF/Blue/R/F

♥ Superstars: almonds, figs, maca, cashews, coconut, cacao

> *Coconut butter...*
> is not the same thing as coconut oil. Coconut butter is a divine, raw, whole food that also contains the meat of the coconut. Another way to explain the difference between coconut butter versus coconut oil is to think of the difference in viscosity between peanut butter and peanut oil. Coconut butter can be found in most health food stores.

 Dark Chocolate Mint Cookies

Are you ready for something ridiculously exciting? Then make up a batch of these totally delish, vitalizing, nourishing, raw cookies that only take 5 minutes to make!

- ½ cup *each:* raw almonds and raisins
- ¼ cup raw cashews
- 3 tablespoons raw cacao powder
- 1 tablespoon raw agave nectar
- 2 teaspoons vanilla
- 1 teaspoon mint extract
- ⅛ teaspoon sea salt

Blend all of the ingredients in a food processor until the mixture is in fine crumbs and very sticky. Remove 1-tablespoon bits of the mixture, roll into balls, and form into cookies. These will store, refrigerated in an airtight container, for a month.

Makes 12 cookies (6 servings)/GF/SF/R/Blue/F/30 Minutes or Under!

♥ Superstars: almonds, cashews, cacao

Blueberry Coconut Ice Box Bars

Here's a healthy treat that will soothe your taste buds and simultaneously make you feel like a superhero!

- ¾ cup raw cashews
- ¼ cup plus 2 tablespoons raw agave nectar
- 3 cups blueberries, fresh or frozen
- ¼ cup plus 1 tablespoon fresh lemon juice
- ¼ cup raw coconut butter
- 1 tablespoon vanilla extract
- ¼ teaspoon sea salt

1. Soak the cashews in water for 8-12 hours or overnight. Drain and set aside.

2. In a food processor or blender, combine the cashews with the agave nectar. Blend until as smooth as possible. Add the remaining ingredients and, once again, blend until as smooth as humanly possible. (You'll forgive my redundancy when you taste these.)

3. Pour/scrape into a medium-sized glass baking dish and even out the top so that the surface is smooth and flat. Cover and freeze for several hours, until hard enough to cut.

4. Cut into 16 squares. Serve ice cold on plates, right out of the freezer.

Makes 16 bars
GF/SF/Blue/R/F

♥ Superstars: blueberries, lemon, coconut

Heavenly Raw Chocolate Sauce

This delectable sauce is perfect for those times when you want a quick, easy, vitalizing treat that makes your knees go completely weak. You know, one of *those* times.

- ¼ cup plus 1 tablespoon raw agave nectar
- 2 tablespoons *each:* raw cacao powder and "Sweet Almond Milk" (p. 56), or other nondairy milk
- 1 tablespoon *each:* raw maca powder and coconut oil
- 1 teaspoon vanilla extract
- ⅛ teaspoon sea salt

Serving suggestion:
- 2 cups *each:* banana chunks and fresh strawberries

1. Blend all of the ingredients (except for the fruit) in a blender or food processor until smooth. Serve immediately, or refrigerate for a thicker sauce.

2. Use as a dip for the fresh fruit or drizzle over anything else you can dream up. This will keep, refrigerated in an airtight container, for several weeks. Once refrigerated, this sauce will become thicker and more fudge-like in consistency. Which is also very exciting—obviously.

Serves 4/GF/SF/Blue/R
30 Minutes or Under!

♥ Superstars: cacao, almonds, maca, coconut

Cacao-Cacao Chip Cookies

Can you imagine indulging in chocolate-chocolate chip cookies that taste delicious, take 10 minutes to make, and completely nourish your body? Luckily, you don't have to imagine—whip up a batch of these babies and make it a reality!

- ½ cup *each:* raw cashews and raw almonds
- 5 dried figs (heaping ½ cup figs), stems removed
- 2 tablespoons *each:* raisins and raw cacao powder
- 1 tablespoon *each:* vanilla and raw agave nectar
- ¼ teaspoon sea salt
Add last: 1 tablespoon cacao nibs

1. In a food processor, combine all of the ingredients (except for the cacao nibs). Blend until the mixture is in coarse crumbs and very sticky.

2. Transfer to a bowl and stir in the cacao nibs. With your hands, form into small balls and then flatten into cookies. That's all there is to it—they're now ready to eat! These cookies will store, refrigerated in an airtight container, for several weeks or more.

Makes about one dozen cookies (6 servings)
GF/SF/Blue/R/F
30 Minutes or Under!

♥ Superstars: cashews, almonds, figs, cacao

Menu Suggestions

This is the part where I help you organize your favorite recipes and turn them into balanced meals. Whether you need to feed the kiddos or you're planning a Thai feast for friends, this chapter has the skinny on what's what. Feel free to use these suggestions as is, or modify them with your preferences.
Happy planning—and eating!

Power Brunch:
Maca My Day (p. 53) or Eye Love You Smoothie (p. 48)
Power Pancakes (p. 42) with Kick Acai Strawberry Sauce (p. 161)
Sweet and Simple Glazed Tempeh (p. 143)
Sweet and Savory Breakfast Fritters (p. 45)
Basic Grilled Asparagus (p. 126)

Meals in a Glass (Healthy Breakfasts On the Go):
Dark Chocolate Raspberry Shake (p. 47)
Eye Love You Smoothie (p. 48)
Spicy Pumpkin Pie Shake (p. 49)
Sunrise Smoothie (p. 50)
Strawberry Vanilla Milkshake (p. 51)
Blueberry Bliss Smoothie (p. 51)
Acai The Light Smoothie (p. 52)
Maca My Day (p. 53)

Kid-Friendly Recipes:
Power Pancakes (p. 42)
Breakfast Quinoa (p. 43)
Frozen Bananas (p. 46)
Dark Chocolate Raspberry Shake (p. 47)
Eye Love You Smoothie (p. 48)
Spicy Pumpkin Pie Shake (p. 49)
Sunrise Smoothie (p. 50)
Strawberry Vanilla Milkshake (p. 51)
Blueberry Bliss Smoothie (p. 51)

Acai The Light Smoothie (p. 52)
Maca My Day (p. 53)
Lemon-Lime Aid (p. 54)
Pineapple Hibiscus Cooler (p. 55)
Sweet Almond Milk (p. 56)
Miso Healthy Dressing (p. 58)
Guilt-Free Ranch Dressing (p. 59)
Sweet 'N Sour Sauce (p. 65)
Lemon Asparagus Quinoa Toss (p. 137)
10 Minute Kalesadillas (p. 147)
Feel Fabulous Noodles (p. 148-149)
Smoky One Pot Beans and Rice (p. 150)
Our Daily Pizza (p. 151)
Feel Good Mac 'N Cheese (p. 156)
Springtime Celebration Salad (p. 116)
Basic Grilled Asparagus (p. 126)
Garlic Lover's Broccoli (p. 127)
Roasted Rosemary Butternut Squash (p. 86)
Fast and Forbidden Fried Rice (p. 91)
Sweet 'N Spicy Turmeric Popcorn (p. 70)
Zesty Lemon Kale Chips (p. 71)
Sprouted Dipper Chips (p. 73)
Spicy Moroccan Sweet Potato Fries (p. 74)
Rawcho Cheese Dip (p. 75)
Green Velvet Guacamole (p. 77)
Supercharged Hummus (p. 78)
Vegan Cheese Sticks (p. 80-81)
Raw Cinnamon Rolls (p. 81)
Lemon Fig Balls (p. 82)
Gingersnap Nuggets (p. 83)
Simple Sesame Miso Soup (p. 101)
Ginger Lime Carrot Soup (minus the cayenne) (p. 102)
15 Minute White Bean and Kale Soup (p. 103)
Grilled Cheese Greatness (p. 112)
Key Lime Pie with Coconut Ginger Crust (p. 158)
Rawkin Superfood Truffles (p. 159)
Pineapple Right-Side-Up Cake (p. 160)
Kick Acai Strawberry Sauce (p. 161)
Mango Paradise Bars (p. 162)

Raw Carob Maca Chocolate (p. 163)
Raw Cacao Superfood Pie (p. 164-165)
Blueberry Coconut Ice Box Bars (p. 166)
Heavenly Raw Chocolate Sauce with fresh fruit (p. 167)

Uber Quick Entrées in a Pinch:
10 Minute Kalesadillas (p. 147)
Feel Good Mac 'N Cheese (p. 156)
Grilled Cheese Greatness (p. 112)
Our Daily Pizza (p. 151)
Lemon Asparagus Quinoa Toss (p. 137)
Springtime Stir-fry (p. 136)
Perfect Tabouli (p. 117)
Hungarian Chickpeas (p. 146)
Chicky Chickadillas (p. 108-109)
BBQ Chickadillas (p. 110-111)

Healthy Comfort Food Dinner (Option One):
Happiness Bowl (p. 140-141)
Basic Grilled Asparagus (p. 126)

Healthy Comfort Food Dinner (Option Two):
Feel Good Mac 'N Cheese (p. 156)
Garlic Lover's Broccoli (p. 127)
Green salad with Guilt-Free Ranch Dressing (p. 59)

Healthy Comfort Food Dinner (Option Three):
Grilled Cheese Greatness (p. 112)
Spicy Moroccan Sweet Potato Fries (p. 74)
Green salad with Onion Dill Miso Dressing (p. 63)

Healthy Comfort Food Dinner (Option Four):
Vegan Cheese Sticks (p. 80-81)
Holy Shiitake Lentil Soup (p. 100)
Asparagus Walnut Sunshine Salad (p. 118)

Ultra-Quick Comfort Food Dinner:
Our Daily Pizza (p. 151)
15 Minute White Bean and Kale Soup (p. 103)

One Dish Meals:
Lemon Asparagus Quinoa Toss (p. 137)
Happiness Bowl (p. 140-141)
Smoky One Pot Beans and Rice (p. 150)
Uptown Salad (p. 114-115)
Mediterranean Pasta Salad (p. 120)
Fresh and Fast Thai Tofu Bowl (p. 134-135)
10 Minute Kalesadillas (p. 147)
Springtime Stir-fry (p. 136)
Tropical Curry Slurry (p. 139)

Healthy Thai Feast:
Fresh Summer Rolls (p. 92-93)
Thai Coconut Treasures Soup (p. 104)
Fresh and Fast Thai Tofu Bowl (p. 134-135)
Mango Paradise Bars (p. 162)

Healthy Holiday Celebration Feast:
Citrus Beets with Maple Orange Walnuts (p. 128-129)
Springtime Celebration Salad (p. 116)
Ginger Lime Carrot Soup (p. 102)
Roasted Rosemary Butternut Squash (p. 86)
Happiness Bowl (p. 140-141)
Raw Cacao Superfood Pie (p. 164-165)

Asian Dinner One:
Fresh Shiitake Sesame Spring Rolls (p. 96-97)
Green Tea and Pineapple Rice with Coconut Tofu (p. 144-145)
Key Lime Pie with Coconut Ginger Crust (p. 158)

Asian Dinner Two:
Ginger Lime Carrot Soup (p. 102)
Baby greens with toasted almonds and Miso Healthy Dressing (p. 58)

Fast and Forbidden Fried Rice (p. 91)
Mango Paradise Bars (p. 162)

Asian Dinner Three:
Umeboshi Sesame Kale (p. 123)
Feel Fabulous Noodles (p. 148-149)
Blueberry Coconut Ice Box Bars (p. 166)

Raw Foods Feast:
Rawcho Cheese Dip (p. 75) with crudités (raw vegetables)
Large vegetable salad with Lemon Ginger Miso Dressing (p. 61)
Bold Lime Kale Krunchers (p. 76)
Mango Paradise Bars (p. 162) and/or Rawkin Superfood Truffles (p. 159)

Japanese Dinner:
Simple Sesame Miso Soup (p. 101)
Baby greens with Ume Sesame Dressing (p. 62)
Miso Sesame Edamame (p. 94)
Umeboshi Rice (p. 88)

Mediterranean Feast:
Perfect Tabouli (p. 117)
Mediterranean Pasta Salad (p. 120)
Sprouted Dipper Chips (p. 73)
Babaganoush (p. 72) and/or Supercharged Hummus (p. 78)

Mexican Fiesta Feast (Option One):
Springtime Celebration Salad (p. 116)
Green Velvet Guacamole (p. 77) with blue corn tortilla chips
Black-eyed Pea and Potato Tacos (p. 132-133)
Mango Paradise Bars (p. 162) or Raw Cacao Superfood Pie (p. 164-165)

Mexican Fiesta Feast (Option Two):
Baby greens with Guilt-Free Ranch Dressing (p. 59)
Crunchy Tempeh Fajitas (p. 106-107) with Pretty Pico (p. 66)
Green Velvet Guacamole (p. 77) with blue corn tortilla chips
Heavenly Raw Chocolate Sauce (add cinnamon and cayenne for extra Mexican flair) with bananas and strawberries (p. 167)

Recommendations and Resources

Fabulous Prepared Foods:

• *GT Synergy kombucha:* Addictively delicious and revitalizing? Yes, please! My favorites are the strawberry, guava, gingerberry, gingerade, and passionberry.

• *Earth Café:* Delicious raw vegan cheesecakes that are made from great ingredients—my favorites are the lemon, raspberry, and strawberry. www.earthcafetogo.com

• *Alvarado Street whole wheat tortillas:* These are made with a combination of whole wheat flour and sprouted wheat berries for a very healthy, 100% whole-grain (yet soft) tortilla experience!

• *Vegenaise Reduced Fat Vegan Mayo*: I love this stuff! It's made with flax and olive oils, and is delicious despite being much lower in fat than most other varieties of mayonnaise.

• *Daiya vegan cheese:* A revolution for cheezy vegans like me! I order mine at veganessentials.com, but you can also find it in many health food stores.

• *Nancy's soy yogurt:* This stuff is incredibly vitalizing! It's one of those foods I can just "feel" in my system right away—I think it's all the fresh cultures and great ingredients. I order the quart-sized yogurts by the case (from my local health food store) as they're very inexpensive that way.

• *Ezekiel 4:9 sprouted grain bread (Food For Life brand):* This flourless bread is just about as healthy as it gets! My personal favorite is the sesame. It's available in the frozen section of health food stores (and many supermarkets).

• *Mary's Gone Crackers "Sticks and Twigs"* are a yummy whole food snack for on-the-go munching. Their crackers are also made with great ingredients. Try either with guacamole or avocado for a quick, satisfying mini-meal.

• **Woodstock Farms frozen sliced shiitake mushrooms:** They taste wonderfully fresh, so I can only imagine that they're using very high quality mushrooms. You can find them in most health food stores.

• **Eden brand foods:** If I were to use a packaged soymilk, Eden would be my choice. Their quality foods always impress me as being made with a higher awareness and care.

• **Amy's frozen foods:** If you're in a time crunch, it's hard to find a better choice as far as frozen foods go. They're always vegetarian and usually organic. Plus, they offer a plethora of vegan and gluten-free options.

• **Chocalive! raw vegan truffles:** These are divine! My favorite is the mint chocolate chip.

• **Steaz green tea and blueberry stevia-sweetened beverage:** This is such a delicious splurge, made even better by the fact that it's calorie-free!

• **KeVita coconut probiotic drinks:** I'm in love with the strawberry acai version of this drink! Sweetened only with stevia and chock-full of probiotics, vitamins, and electrolytes, this is one of my very favorite guilt-free indulgences.

• **Foods Alive:** Their raw maca and cacao powders are divine!

Books:

• **Radiant Health, Inner Wealth**: This is the 2nd edition of my complete guide to wellness, including over 240 color-coded recipes that will keep you eating well for a very long time! www.RadiantHealth-InnerWealth.com

• **The Two-Week Wellness Solution: The Fast Track to Permanent Weight Loss and Vitality!**: My two-week plan is a great way to detoxify your body while still eating delicious foods. www.RadiantHealth-InnerWealth.com

• **The New Whole Foods Encyclopedia by Rebecca Wood:** This wonderful resource contains everything you could ever want to know about whole foods. www.amazon.com

• *Local Wild Life by Katrina Blair:* This book is a treasure of delicious living foods, written with love. www.TurtleLakeRefuge.org

• *The Thrive Diet by Brendan Brazier:* Inspired recipes and expert advice from a vegan ironman triathlete. www.amazon.com

• *Vegan Bodybuilding and Fitness by Robert Cheeke:* An excellent guide for beginners or advanced athletes. Robert gives you indispensable information on achieving top performance, using the vegan edge. www.veganbodybuildingbook.com

• *The Happy Herbivore Cookbook by Lindsay S. Nixon:* A great resource for fat-free and lowfat vegan dishes that are easy to prepare and full of nutrients.

• *eat, drink, and be vegan by Dreena Burton:* A beautifully written cookbook, filled with tempting vegan dishes and helpful tips.

Kitchen Resources:

• *Pampered Chef garlic press:* You don't even have to peel the cloves—so convenient!

• *Excalibur food dehydrator:* The best food dehydrator I know of. I have the big daddy (nine tray model) and love it!

• *SoyaPower soymilk maker:* A great investment—ours paid for itself in about four months.

• *Cuisinart food processors:* I've always had great luck with this brand of food processors.

• *Benriner spiralizer:* Fun for making angelhair-like strands of carrots, beets, potatoes, or zucchini. A great tool for raw foods (and kid-friendly veggies).

• *Vitamix blender:* A great way to make the smoothest of the smooth fruit drinks, nut butters, soups, and more.

Recommended Restaurants:

- **Chicago Diner (Chicago, Illinois)**: Some of the yummiest vegan food I've ever had! I also love how there are lots of truly healthful, whole-food choices on their menu. Dishes I've had and loved include their raw lime cheesecake, quinoa tostadas, and enchiladas.

- **McFoster's Natural Kind (Omaha, Nebraska):** Very vegan-friendly—plus, they grow many of their own vegetables. Be sure to get the "Celestial Bananas" for dessert!

- **Himalayan Kitchen (Durango, Colorado)**: Lovely staff and delicious food from Nepal and India. They offer several vegan dishes. Especially good are the Vegan Kumari Tarkaari, Kuchumber Salad, and Vegetarian Mo-mos.

- **Udupi Café (Indianapolis, Indiana):** This vegetarian restaurant has many delicious vegan options as well. So yummy!

- **Millennium Restaurant (San Francisco, California):** Gourmet vegan cuisine at its finest!

- **Watercourse (Denver, Colorado):** Anything on the menu can be made vegan—and everything I've tried here is delicious! However, my top picks are the "Po Boy" sandwich, mashed potatoes and gravy, and salads with maple dijon dressing.

- **Sunflower Vegetarian Restaurant (Vienna, Virginia):** Mostly vegan and very yummy, I can't help ordering the "Kung Pao Chicken" (vegan) and avocado lemon pie every time I visit!

- **Café 118 Degrees (Winter Park, Florida):** This vegan, raw foods restaurant is incredible! Everything I've tried has been just amazing. My favorites, however, are the raw lasagna, hummus-type dip with flax crackers, stuffed poblanos with mole sauce, cacao-mint-chip ice cream, and blueberry cheesecake.

- **Café Gratitude (San Francisco, California):** Two words—vegan tiramisu.

- **End of The Line Café (Pensacola, Florida):** An all-vegan restaurant, I recommend stopping by for their Sunday brunches or Thursday night dinners.

• **_Tasty Harmony (Fort Collins, CO):_** This restaurant has great vegan whole-food selections as well as many raw options. Their nachos are a local favorite.

• **_Daily Juice (Austin, Texas):_** An all-vegan (and mostly raw) café, this place really impressed me! I loved their raw Caesar salad, eggplant "bacon" sandwich, and plethora of raw chocolates. Divine!

• **_Candle 79 (New York):_** This all-vegan restaurant is considered by many to be the best spot in the northeast.

• **_Raw Can Roll Café (Douglassville, PA):_** Try the vegan tostadas, spring rolls, and raw pasta.

• **_Wild Cow (Nashville, TN):_** A vegetarian restaurant where almost everything on the menu can be made vegan (and gluten-free).

• **_Mary's Secret Garden (Ventura, CA):_** Organic, vegan cuisine—try the Spanish Grande Burrito, Thai Yellow Curry Stew & Raw Chocolate Pecan Pie.

• **_Real Food Daily (Southern CA and expanding):_** An all-vegan, organic establishment with an amazing menu!

Index

D

E

F

G

I

J

K

L

M

N

O

P

S

U

*May you enjoy radiance and vitality
on every level . . . for life!*
♥ ♥ ♥ ♥

www.RadiantHealth-InnerWealth.com